TREASURES OF THE MIND

Edited by

Kelly Deacon

First published in Great Britain in 1999 by
ANCHOR BOOKS
Remus House,
Coltsfoot Drive,
Woodston,
Peterborough, PE2 9JX
Telephone (01733) 898102

All Rights Reserved

Copyright Contributors 1999

HB ISBN 1 85930 790 6
SB ISBN 1 85930 795 7

FOREWORD

Anchor Books is a small press, established in 1992, with the aim of promoting readable poetry to as wide an audience as possible.

We hope to establish an outlet for writers of poetry who may have struggled to see their work in print.

The poems presented here have been selected from many entries. Editing proved to be a difficult task and as the Editor, the final selection was mine.

I trust this selection will delight and please the authors and all those who enjoy reading poetry.

Kelly Deacon
Editor

CONTENTS

Thorns And Roses	Mary Petrie	1
Changing Times	Joan E Bartlett	2
Gentle Wind	William E Stimson	2
The Curragraigue Air	H Hubbard	3
How Much Do You Love Me?	Wilma J Gravenor	4
My Child	Mary Cruz	4
Seasons	M Boey	5
My Avon Garden	J M Stoles	6
Through The Eyes Of A Child	T N McCarroll	6
The Fish Bowl	Joan A Bidwell	7
Happiness	Edna E Pine	8
To My Love	Betty J Bevan	8
What Would I Do?	Liz Dicken	9
The Welsh Flag	Elwynne	9
Yellow Trumpets	Nicky Wharton	10
The Stray Cat	Gordon Butchers	10
Country Skills	Stella Williamson	11
Kent	C H De Meza	12
Please Will You Buy My Lovely Flowers	Barbara Towes	13
Deus Vobiscum	Daphne Kirkpatrick	14
Ode To A Husband	Rosemary Joan Smith	14
Hepatitis	Linda Williams	15
Winter's Poem	A Fry	16
1951	K Ward	17
Magpies	Gwyneth M Bere	17
Does It Really Matter?	Phyllis Ing	18
That's How It Is	Wendy Watkin	19
Senseless	Wendy P Lukasik	20
Life	M Moore	20
Childhood Pleasure	Milly Saunders	21
I Know This	P Taylor	22
Picturesque Cornwall	Julie Tippett	22
June Past	Susan Naile	23
Things To Come	April M A Came	24
The Isles Of Scilly	G Futer	24

Sitting On The Lap Of God	C J Walls	25
Bird Life	M Wevill	26
Doggy (Jamie's) Thoughts	David Allen	26
Gods And Goddesses Poem	Ben Hughes	27
The Old Days	L McCubbin	28
Ode To Kilve Beach	V C Matthews	29
Again	Damon Naile	30
Hail To Spring	Marjorie B Dixon	30
Choice?	Christine Wilson	31
The Reasons I Love You	Robin Grigsby	32
Home Truths	Geoffrey Elgar	33
The Old Railway	Anna Moore	34
The Patient Patient	D Thorpe	35
Dream Time	Juliette Matthews	36
The Old Horse	Priscilla Winn	36
In Bed	Elizabeth Hibbert	37
Portland	Mamorald	38
Es	Kate Brown	39
Soul Growth	Dolly Little	40
The Glove	G J Porter	41
The Emperor's New Clothes	H Lomas	42
Embers Left Of Passion's Tide	Isobel Sangster	43
It's Where You Finish	Maisie Trussler	44
Future Journey	J Feld	44
The Flood	Stacie Flood	45
That Tree	Brian Frost	46
Sheba	P Hughes	47
Compromise	Linda Walker	47
Mum And Dad December 1998	Garry J Casalinie	48
Lawnmower Symphony	N Mason	48
Love Has Passed (The Robin, Never)	Christopher Irwin Poynter	49
Jemima Holly's Brolly	M Fowler	50
Who, Me?	Joan E Edney	51
His Love Is So Great	E Squire	52
Untitled	L Fairclough	52
County Colours	D Garlick	53
Bathroom Scales -Weight	Anna P Aldridge	54

Nightmary	Anthony D Parker	54
As Drawn By Lowry	Janet Bloomfield	55
Talking Flowers	T Splitt	56
Dawning	Patricia Bull	56
Superstition Or Common Sense	May Cowan	57
The Taxman Cometh	E A Hutchison	58
Mice	Siobhan Anderson	59
Heaven	Nicola Walker	59
Mankind's Madness	David Strauss Steer	60
Highland Deer	Alice Devita	60
Lochgelly	A Cowan	61
A Stranger's Smile	Barry Cooper	62
Whoops!	Beulah Thompson	62
Walking Backwards In Asda	W Oliphant	63
Taking The Biscuit!	Joyce Hockley	64
Spring Has Sprung	Margaret Findlay	65
Incredibly Alone Today	Anne Beattie	66
Grandma Is Gone	Cassandra Simms-Sawyers	67
Bedtime Story	Edwina Ainscough	68
A Log Cabin	J M Peek	68
Christmas	J Mulholland	69
When The Rains Came	George Findlay	70
Memories Of Summer	Ann Stevenson	71
The Ice-Cream	James Cartmell	72
Big Brother	Gemma Cole	73
A Dream	Grace Brown	74
All The Roofs Of London	Ian Dixon	74
The Nurse	The Portonian	75
Dalmatian	Aimee Upton	76
Mother's Day	E V Salmon	76
Lacock In Summer	Doris Cowie	77
Why?	Ian McFarlane	78
Eden	Maureen Cropley	78
First Flight	P Bates	79
God's Missing Bit	Glennis Horne	80
Too Late	Jill Reeve	81
The Media	J McElroy	82
Thoughts Of An Older Woman	Constance Wateridge	83

A Twin And Mother Of Twins	Declan O'Sullivan	84
Sad Desecration Of An Island Roundabout	George W Lansbury	85
Nona	M J Boden	86
Grandma's Geraniums	J Cook	86
A Far Away Dream	J Darts	87
Urban Expansion	D A Spence-Crawford	88
The Village Green	Winifred Shore	89
For All Of Your Life	Gerald Marsh	90
The Outside Cat	D Price	91
Little Miss Howard	Gavin Stewart	92
The Grandmother Clock	David Whitworth	93
Mrs Bronsmoor	R Tapley	94
Marteg Bridge	Wendy Dedicott	94
Hereford Cider	Ruth Mollon	95
On Holiday But Missing Home	C Growcott	96
Bristol	M E Beale	97
Whisper	Jolana Hoskova	98
The White Flower	Anita E Matthews	99
Old Jack	E Henley	100
Holiday In Exmouth	Ann Harford	101
Heaven's Not What It Seems	M Cobbold	102
All For Nowt	Jane Rennie	103
Dreams Of The Past	Walter Causer	104
The Joys Of Summer	Carol Wright	105
Confusion	Ailsa Baillie	106
At The Crossroads	Matthew Turpin	106
Old England	Wagtail	107
Crash	Ian Jackson	108
Home To Stay	Elizabeth Patterson	109
Camping By Loch Ar'n	Roger Coates Smith	109
Eternity	B Wood	110
Summertime	A Dutschak	110
Mary	Edward Joseph Clark	111
Married Life Is A Wonderful Thing	C Ducker	112
Remember Me	Clare A Lewis	113
Ennui Des Enfants	Frank Sutton	114

3rd March 1972 (Aftermath)	P Mannion	114
Toddler Trip	Cathy Saunders	115
I Do Notice	Lauren Nield	116
Mad Cow	Alice Sanders	117
Your Star Shines On Me	Clive Louis Turvey	118
We Are The Lucky Ones	Joan King	119
Pigs	E Collins	120
Crackerman	A Howard	121
To Goodwood By Way Of Wisborough Green	Audrey Euangeline	122
Colne Valley Waters	Jack Judd	123
A Sense Of Timing	Phoenix Martin	124
Yellow Dogs	M Eissa	124
Roll Up	A Clough	125
Relations And Rabbits	Clare McAfee	126
Morgan The Shepherd And His Wife	Lucy Gallilee	127
What Is It About You?	Angela McLaughlin	127
Assertiveness	Sue Barnes	128
The Place In Which We Live	M M Forshaw	129
A Birthday Blessing	J Knott	130
My Thoughts	Jade Hughes	131
Autumn	Pamela J New	132
My Rocking Chair	Eileen Handley	132
Woods	G Nussbaum	133
Solitude	Margaret E Preston	134
My Love For You	Margaret Jean Wilcock	134
Truth	David James	135
Snowman	Kathy Watson	135
The Bad Chair	John F McCartney	136
Hands	John McGowan	137
Amoral Dilemma?	Geraldine McIlmurray	138
The Butterfly	L Barnes	138
Invention	Nell Thompson	139
Winter On The Farm	Isobel Crumley	140
Mouth Like A Rose	Millicent B Colwell	141
Land Of My Dreams	Lesley Stevenson	142
Come to The Fair	G Emery	143

Victims Of Circumstance	Elizabeth A Rice	144
Lighthouse	Gemma Guymer	145
East Anglia	Sally A Swain	146
Casablanca	Romana Bartosiak	146
A Message From Mom	Lynn Jean Barry	147
Sunday	M Walker	147
Mr Nobody	Joyce Mussett	148
To A Dragonfly	James V Hooton	149
Yesterday	I D Welch	149
Mystery Coach Tour	Sheila Town	150
Silent Prayer	J R Reading	151
A Step Wanting	Susan Roberts	152
Words	Margaret Vinall-Burnett	153

THORNS AND ROSES

'A rose by any other name . . .'
But what of the rose's thorn?
Would it pierce so harshly
If it was not called thorn?

And then my Lord,
Who on this Earth was born;
And lived, and died,
And for me bore such scorn.

No rose for him; a crown of thorn
They made him wear,
Upon a cross, his body torn,
Then left him, hanging there.

The end of him, they thought,
And yet my Lord is not so easily struck low;
For the rose you prune back hardest,
Will the greatest beauty show.

But it was not the Jews
'Twas God who did this thing:
Raised Jesus to great glory
To rescue me, and you, from sin.

And so the Lord's victorious
No more the crown of thorn.
After three days in the tomb,
Jesus rose.

Mary Petrie

CHANGING TIMES

Then:

We couldn't wait to go out
No matter what the weather
If it rained or snowed
We had to get together
Because we were outcasts
Teenagers no less
Together we identified
We had to progress

Now:

We can't wait to get home
To our slippers and cocoa
Our Soaps on TV
The streets are no-go
Because we are old
As we all will be
These words are for everyone
For you and for me.

Joan E Bartlett

GENTLE WIND

I heard gentle wind you come once more
As you softly closed the bedroom door.
I have a message yet again
For she whom I adore, I fear, in vain.

As you open her casement wide
Push the coloured curtain aside.
And when you see her sleeping there
Kiss her cheeks and ruffle her hair.

Tell her I'll love her for evermore
Tell her I'll love her for evermore
Evermore - evermore.
She must be the loveliest lady that you ever saw - ever saw.
Tell her I'll love her for evermore.

William E Stimson

THE CURRAGRAIGUE AIR

The Curragraigue air should be bottled and sold,
But given to youngsters,
The frail, and the old.

The Curragraigue air is a tonic so fine,
It blows from the mountain,
It's free - and it's mine.

The Curragraigue air is the morning's first bite,
Its taste such a welcome
With dawn's fragile light.

The Curragraigue air is my food for the day,
It satisfies hunger
In its own special way.

The Curragraigue air is the glass in my hand
It quenches the thirst
And drenches the land!

The Curragraigue air is a spirit unseen;
It always will be
As it always has been.

H Hubbard

How Much Do You Love Me?

Feeling older?
Yes, a little.
Getting greyer?
Yes, a little.
Seem less active?
Yes, a little.
Moving slower?
Yes, a little.
Memory dodgy?
Yes, a little.
Restless sleeping?
Yes, a little.
Feeling isolated?
Yes, a little.
Need some loving?
Yes, a little.
. . . 'Then I'm here for you Grandma -
and I love you lots!'

Wilma J Gravenor

My Child

If I can watch you sleeping,
I will be happy.

If I can watch you waking,
I will see the sun.

If I can watch you laughing,
I have succeeded.

If I have to watch you crying,
I will avenge you.

If I ever find you lonely,
I will ease your pain.

If I have to watch you dying,
I will come with you.

Mary Cruz

SEASONS

Woolly lambs bleating, lovers meeting,
Fleecy clouds drifting. New blooms lifting.
Soft breezes blowing, cattle lowing.
Restless feeling; swallows wheeling,
Must be spring!
Sunshine blazing, people lazing,
Children play in carts of hay.
End of school, keeping cool.
Cold ice-creams, sparkling streams,
Summertime!
Harvest done, mellow sun.
Sheaves of corn, misty morn.
Bright moon shining, days declining.
Autumn's come!
Cold winds blowing, then it's snowing.
Children sliding, cars colliding.
Santa's near, bringing cheer.
Winter's here!

M Boey

MY AVON GARDEN

Water cans and flowerpots
Lay strewn across the lawn
Broken toys are forgotten
From years ago
They are scattered
Behind the potting shed
And birds
Call to one another
Our sundial sits
In the middle of the lawn
And in the evening
Shadows creep across the ground
Birds hop hunting for insects and seeds
And hiding behind the trees
Are small rodents
The sun casts its fiery glow
Across the purple sky.

J M Stoles

THROUGH THE EYES OF A CHILD

I sat alone and could not see,
only that which tormented me.
My senses all had dimmed and died
and I looked at life, and then I cried

The years had passed and left me old,
and I was frightened and I was cold.
But something in the eternal hate,
prompted me to challenge fate.

And I read again my Saviour's words,
and I listened to the singing birds.
I looked again at the changing scene,
I looked again where I had been

I looked at love, gentle and mild
I looked at life, through the eyes of a child.

T N McCarroll (dec'd)

THE FISH BOWL

At evening leafless trees are spread
like pencilled seaweed on a sky
of watery blue and green. Think I
(strange fancies passing through my head)
Suppose that it should really be
water, and suppose that we
to eyes that peer above the brim
are darting round as fishes swim
that think their pretty bowl a sea.
And high above our little sphere
are bending mighty Seraph wings
in casual curiosity,
and starry eyes pierce through to see
the curious little water things
that make their weeds appear as tall
as Heaven's trees, they are so small.
'Yes, yes, the Lord Almighty keeps them here
and is particular that they are fed.
He says some even ask for daily bread.
He sets great store by them, it seems' - a sigh
rippled the weeds - 'though He alone knows why'

Joan A Bidwell

HAPPINESS

Happiness is a precious thing
It cannot be bought
We make it ourselves and spread it around
Like a gardener who prepares the ground
And plants seeds to grow into beautiful flowers
So our actions result in happy hours
No planning ahead is required
But just our will, inspired
By right-thinking, devoid of all selfishness,
Wanting to make others happy,
And this rebounds -
Like wells springing from the ground,
Fountains of joy appear
And happiness flourishes everywhere.

Edna E Pine

TO MY LOVE

I stood with you one happy sunlit day
Upon a tiny bridge o'er rippling stream
And told you of my love
'Neath sky supreme.
A silver winged seagull soared above
And trees made silhouettes against the blue -
And then I knew
As long as nature's wings caress the earth
And springtime's young green leaves are bathed in dew,
As long as there is life
I'll cherish you.

Betty J Bevan

WHAT WOULD I DO?

What would I do if the aliens came?
At first I'd stand and stare in disbelief,
I'd run for cover to a safer haven,
not knowing what my destiny might be.
Perhaps there would be no point, perhaps they have already read
    my mind?
What do they want? Will they take me away?
I think there is no choice, with no brainpower left to call my own,
    my mind a total blank . . .
I'll make a quick decision now! While there
    still is time . . . or is there?
Never till now have I loved this world so much,
    and yet . . .
Felt compelled to leave by some
    unseen mystic power . . .

Liz Dicken

THE WELSH FLAG

My holidays when young were spent in Wales.
My loved Welsh grandma told me many tales,
Of Merlin, myths and legends and folklore.
So many tales - I always asked for more.
She told me how St George, so brave and bold
Had killed the fierce red dragon and she told
Me that is why we have St George's cross
On flag of Wales - why dragon is embossed
On flag and drape hanging in the hall.
'Twas to remind male heirs when they are called -
They fight for Wales, Great Britain and St George.

Elwynne

YELLOW TRUMPETS

Attention to detail dear
It's blatantly clear
Is a gift you do not possess
Your impression is a mess

The leaves should be simple
But they bend and dimple
Casting dark and light
This doesn't look quite right

Trumpets tall and bold
A beauty to behold
Sketched lightly on my lap
They appear to have lost their sap

There must be a technique
To capturing this mystique
The result will be quite spectacular
When viewed through my camera

Nicky Wharton

THE STRAY CAT

Poor old ginger Tom
A poor old stray,
When I try to stroke him
He turns and runs away.

Scavenging in the litter bins
For something to eat,
No home to go to
A life on the street.

Out in all weathers
Both day and night,
Fur all matted
He looks a pitiful sight.

Poor old ginger Tom
May you safely roam,
If you would only let me
I'd like to take you home.

Gordon Butchers

COUNTRY SKILLS

Old tailboards fed the wheelwright's fire,
And elm that came from some old wheel;
And thus was made a metal tire
For carts of oak, and ash, and deal.
Wagons, ready to be driven
By Carter's who their horses clothed
In bells, and bows of crimson ribbon,
And harness brasses, shining gold.
The tranter with his jogging horse
Would carry merchandise and mail;
Might see a hedger on his course,
Or those erecting a farm rail.
So many tasks these men could do,
Make garden sticks from rods of ash;
Could ditch, lay hedges; good folks who,
If called, a cottage roof would patch.
With bat and hazel spears, the roof
With wheaten reed had once been laid;
A skill, an art, the thatcher's proof
That he was master of his trade.

Stella Williamson

KENT

Kent was once a Kingdom,
It had a Christian queen.
But still it's no use thinking,
On things which may have been.

Today Kent is a county,
Our Garden so they say,
With wheat and hops and apples,
And stacks and stacks of hay.

They breed sheep down on the marsh,
Making wool and English lamb.
Let's stop and get a pot of tea,
With scones and cream and jam.

Dover is the garden gate,
Where people come and go.
From places on the continent,
And as far as people know.

Trains run through a tunnel,
Linking Kent with parts of France.
You can go to taste a glass of wine,
Or just to dine and dance.

See Canterbury Cathedral,
The head church in our land.
Explore the ancient city,
It's all there close at hand.

The Meadway towns are great to see,
The dock yard's now on show.
Once they built the Navy's ships,
Designed to beat the foe.

Margate is a nice resort,
With Folkestone close behind.
And you can drive the Ashford ring road,
If you are brave and have the mind.

C H De Meza

PLEASE WILL YOU BUY MY LOVELY FLOWERS?

Please will you buy my lovely flowers
From me?
Don't you see
That I am blind
Please help me
Please be kind
I have no home
Nowhere to go
Please will you buy my lovely flowers?
And give me the help I need so
Lovely flowers for sale
I shout
I can hear a lot of people about
Don't turn away
My life's no fun
When everything is so grey
A coin drops in my basket
Thank you mister I shout
I know it's a man
For he touched my hand
Thank you mister
You're so kind
Oh how I wish I could see you
But I can imagine you in my mind

Barbara Towes

DEUS VOBISCUM

Are you
a Saint, I wonder?
Little man with
a gnarled, old stick,
An angel in disguise perhaps.

Why does he pause at our bench,
Look kindly down, with eyes
of a remarkable blue?
Close-fitting hunting cap
slightly askew, bird of
passage, passing through,
he quotes in Latin
'God be with you.'

Then as he melts into
the midday flow,
the Sacring bell's high notes
ring sharp and clear,
Those who have ears to hear,
Deus Vobiscum.

Daphne Kirkpatrick

ODE TO A HUSBAND

One who has stood by me through the years
Shared my laughter, dreams and fears
Without whom life would be so bleak
Although now it's reached its peak.

No grunts or moans to do a task
Always willing to help when asked
Only trouble he thinks he's God
But 'He' doesn't sleep in just a nod.

Loveable, brainy, great mathematician
Finding in me no competition
We work our years out calm and thrifty
Because he wants to live till he's 150.

We laugh a lot and have great fun
And when our spell on earth is done
I hope in peace we'll be together
Letting his spirit roam forever.

Rosemary Joan Smith

HEPATITIS

I woke at 4am feeling real.
I had been under the influence
of a clichéd Niagara of pain,
which I breathed through
and entered a cavern
of spiky boulders.
They promised I could be
under the influence of pethidine
if the morphine
didn't work.
But I woke up, feeling real,
washed, drank tea,
and wrote this.
In room 34, QA Hospital,
the doctor talks of 'Liver derangement'.
'Best lock it up in an asylum,' I quip.
Then I discover that Ingrid, in room 35,
has psychiatric nurses as constant companions
and is also ill.

Linda Williams

WINTER'S POEM

Sail boats 'n' rough water,
Robin, carrion crow,
Driftwood 'n' tide,
Driftwood 'n' tide,
These are the things of Winter.

Sand bang 'n' scavenge,
Driftwood 'n' tide,
Driftwood 'n' tide.
Of distant summer,
And Noah's great rainbow,
These are the things of Winter.

Spirit, gale, and empty prom.
Forecast 'n' blow,
Forecast 'n' blow,
When fallen colour,
Poppies remember,
You virgin snow,
You virgin snow,
Then carol 'n' dance, carol 'n' dance,
Whilst wrapping your paper, wrapping your paper,
For a child is born to us, a Son is given to us,
Oh berries red, 'n' holly green, beside our firelight,
Warm and welcoming come light,
Now that these are the days of Winter.

A Fry

1951

Rolling white clouds in a blue sky
Flowers in abundance
Smells that remind us of long ago
I often wonder why
Sounds that whisper in your ear
Love that swells your heart
Anything is not easy
There are thoughts not to fear
A church spire so tall
At last we are here
The organ is playing
What a sight I behold
I can hear our song
Only in my mind
Yes I remember this was our year.

K Ward

MAGPIES

Propeller wings of magpies,
Flashing white-tipped
Midst the indigo-black feathers;
Seeking morning prey
Against the darker clouded sky.

While dragons swoop to Earth beneath,
Fearful robins stay still,
Blending in with autumn leaves
Till all danger is passed.

So life goes on, and
Nature resumes her day.

Gwyneth M Bere

DOES IT REALLY MATTER?

Does it really matter that we are not all the same,
That we come from different countries and have a different name,
Does it really matter about the colour of our skin,
Be it yellow, white, black or brown, or even thick or thin?
Does it really matter what others call their God,
Such as Allah, Mohammed, Jesus Christ, or just Our Lord?

      No, these things should not really matter.

But what does really matter is man's inhumanity to Man,
Like throwing thousands of people out of their own homeland.
Like burning all their villages and killing all their men
So that they will never ever see their loved ones again.

      These are the things that matter.

Like seeing the tears and terror on a young child's face
Trudging through a foreign land because he is a different race,
Like raping helpless women at the point of a loaded gun
Watched by a frantic husband, a daughter or a son.

      These are the things that matter.

Will we ever know the answer as to why these things are done?
Why men can be so cruel and heartless because others don't belong
to their own creed and way of life, they call it Ethnic Cleansing,
I don't, I call it ignorance, greed and hatred never-ending.

      Oh I wish I knew the answer to it all.

Phyllis Ing

THAT'S HOW IT IS

Mum's in from shopping,
what does she do?
Pops on the kettle
and makes a brew.

Settles by the fire,
Plonks in a chair,
Puts on the telly
has not a care.

Does a bit of knitting,
Picks up a book
Nearly time for dinner -
must start to cook.

Kids come home,
No peace at all,
The dog starts to bark,
Johnny's playing ball.

Dad comes in
he's had a busy day
Lights up his pipe
and puffs away.

'Will you wash this jumper
I need it tonight.'
'I'll be staying at Suzie's
if that's alright.'

They're needing this,
and doing that,
Mum's life is busy . . .
and that's a fact.

Wendy Watkin

SENSELESS

A shooting it seems
Has happened again,
Which causes much sorrow,
heartache and pain.

Of innocent people
who walk down the street,
And the eyes of a killer
they suddenly meet.

The bullets are fired
without any care.
By a senseless human
with an ice-cold stare.

Who gains great pleasure
in the stream of blood,
which issues from the innocent
and in the street does flood.

Please pray for these ones
And their families too,
As you never know
It could next be you.

Wendy P Lukasik

LIFE

We're all in such a hurry - no time to stop and think -
to cherish 'now', 'the present' and make the important link
with what is past and what's to come and try to make 'the whole',
make sense of life, what it's about, can we fulfil our role?

Time passes by so quickly, we ought to make it count,
we won't be here forever, of that there is no doubt.
To utilise our talents, leave the world a better place -
should be our aim, not rush around, slow down and set the pace.

M Moore

CHILDHOOD PLEASURE

In my early childhood,
   Each day was filled with pleasure,
Visiting grandma's farm was exciting,
   Full of new found adventures.

It was a magical time,
   A young child venturing from town
Embarking on many new experiences,
   Vulnerable, but brave to face danger.

I was introduced to shire horses,
   Oxen, sheep, pigs and to swarms of bees.
There were dogs of different breeds,
   Poultry, ducks, and varieties of geese.

I met farm labourers working in the fields,
   Cutting grass and making hay,
Ploughing, planting, also harvesting,
   Picking grapes, apples, peaches and figs.

Today, I still love and appreciate
   Mother Nature and all her gifts,
Admire my large garden with its many trees,
   But the greatest privilege is to have a hive of bees.

Milly Saunders

I Know This

A buttercup is beautiful
a daisy, seldom praised
trees we take for granted
just like a rainy day,
the passing of the day to night
the glory of the morning light
scents and perfumes on the air,
natures gift
for us to share.
From butterflies and ladybirds
apples, strawberries
and pears,
dew-drops on a rose bush
a breath of clean fresh air,
a fox runs through a valley
see a calf just after birth
the river running gently
as a petal falls to Earth.

P Taylor

Picturesque Cornwall

Ghost town, living citizens,
need a job to stay alive.
Empty shops and silent streets.
Bleak silent moor, engine houses,
monuments of yesteryear.
Standing proud, no longer used.
Fishing boats rotting in port,
fish thrown back rot in the sea.
Farmers, 24 - 7
earning a part-timers wage.

My love, you look to the sea
the fields, the fresh air, the space,
the sun, the sky (black at night).
Come for your two week holiday
and tell us again how much you'd love to live here.

Julie Tippett

JUNE PAST

Sea swishing soothes my head,
Sun warms my mind.
Nostalgia touches my thoughts -
Nudging memories that bind
Us invisibly.

Sand sticks between my toes
Gratingly fine.
Reminiscent of long ago -
Spurring ideas which are mine
But with you in view.

Mountains watch over me,
Looking always down.
But ever caring and secure -
Lifting a fleeting sad frown
Of a June long past.

Seagulls soar on the breeze,
Plaintively pulling
My visions back to the present.
Lying here, the sea lulling
Gentle thoughts of you.

Susan Naile

THINGS TO COME

It is my birthday tomorrow
'Hip, hip, hip hooray.'
For on, such special occasions
It is all, fun and play, for me.
Then, comes the day, after!
When life, comes down, with a bump.
The days, are now filled, with serious things
Like learning, to pass all my exams!
So, I can earn, my living, the best, as I can.
My mother and father, then, will be
Pleased as can be, with little old me!
I'll be able, to get, a wonderful job.
To earn, lots of money, and never, get in debt,
I shall do, my very best, the best, I've done yet!
Then all, will be happy, and carefree.
Reading my results, and congratulating me.
To make, me feel good, as I know, it should,
Oh, happy, happy me!

April M A Came

THE ISLES OF SCILLY

Beyond the coast of Cornwall out in the ocean blue
There lies a chain of islands which call to me and you.
These islands named 'The Scillies' have stood since time began
Amidst the thunderous ocean - all part of nature's plan.

Wild flowers in abundance are growing everywhere.
While in the harbour boats abound to take you here and there.
The weather can be treacherous with mist and wind and rain
But then the clouds will roll away - the sun will shine again.

So if The Scillies call you, be sure that you will find
That nature in her wisdom will fill your heart and mind
With thoughts of all the wonders that she alone can bring
To your time spent in The Scillies, especially in the spring.

G Futer

SITTING ON THE LAP OF GOD

When you struggle with your
faith go to God and sit on His lap.

When life is getting you down go to
God and sit on His lap.

When your circumstances never seem
to change go to God and sit on His lap.

When you have sinned and you need to
repent go to God and sit on His lap.

Go to God and sit on His lap and talk
to Him about your struggle with your faith.
Talk to Him about the life that is
getting you down.
Talk to Him about your circumstances.
Talk to Him about the sin in your life.

As you sit on the lap of God He will listen and
He will take hold of you and cuddle you.

God will always love you and He is always there
for you as you sit on God's lap and talk to Him.

C J Walls

BIRD LIFE

Two little birds sat up in a tree,
They gazed at each other so lovingly,
He said to her 'Do you love me?'
And she replied, 'Oh! Most certainly,'
They started to gather some twigs and some leaves
To build their nest up under the eaves,
And as the days grew longer and longer,
Their love for each other grew stronger and stronger,
And then one day lo! and behold
An addition was made to their happy abode,
Three little eggs were resting there,
Which needed a mother's loving care,
She nestled above them to keep them warm
And shelter them from rain and storm,
While father went out to gather some food,
Mother stayed at home to look after their brood,
And then one day to their greatest joy,
Became the parents of two girls and a boy.

M Wevill

DOGGY (JAMIE'S) THOUGHTS

I could wag my tail and look appealing,
I wonder if I should risk it,
It all depends on how he's feeling,
Dad, can I have a biscuit?

Licking his face and tapping his leg
I often find a winner,
I'd much prefer it, *not* to beg,
Dad, can I have my dinner?

My round black eyes, I use to plead
But I sometimes wish that I could talk,
I'm almost sure he knows what I need,
Dad, can we go for a walk?

I use many ploys, often I bark,
I've also been known to pant,
To me it's all a bit of a lark
But I usually get what I want!

David Allen

GODS AND GODDESSES POEM

Zeus looks down from above,
Aphrodite is the goddess of love.
Hera is Zeus' wife,
In the underworld, Persephone spent
half of her life.

Dionysus is the god of wine,
Apollo's clothes were really fine.
Ares is the god of war,
He would knock Pan on the floor.

Asclepius was the god of medicine,
Hades was the god of sin.
Demeter was goddess of Earth,
Artemis gave every lady birth.

All these gods make up history,
But are there more?
It's a mystery.

Ben Hughes

THE OLD DAYS

Can you imagine in days
gone by
when the roads were quiet
and so the sky.
To hear the buzzing of the
bees
and the rustle of the wind
in the trees.

When the cock was crowing
at the crack of dawn
letting us know that it
was morn.
Time to get started on
that day's work
no time at all for anyone
to shirk.

When errand boys came
riding by
on bikes with baskets, piled
up high.
Whistling a tune that was
all the go
that they had heard at
the theatre show.

Oh for the days of long
ago
when the pace of life was
more slow
and people walking in the
street
would stop and chat to folk
they meet.

Today it's just one long
mad rush
they never seem to keep
in touch.
Do not know whether they
are coming or going
some couldn't care less
what they are doing.

How lucky were we older
folk
who were able to stop and
crack a joke.
It was a hard life and well
we knew
but we did our best and
struggled through.

L McCubbin

ODE TO KILVE BEACH

In my imaginative space, I have become
The sea which effortlessly cleanses the shore.
Receding in form, to an indistinct trace,
In soul, separate, no more.
I emerge from the waves that have held me so near
And fight the passionate squall,
And in the expanse of the spiritual sky
I surrender, the beauty of all.

V C Matthews

AGAIN

And there you go again
Jumping to many conclusions.
Most of them aren't true,
But you,
You believe them anyway.

And there you go again
Rummaging through my belongings.
They're all personal,
Quite dull
But you rummage anyway.

And there you go again
Finding lipstick on my collar.
It's not even there,
Don't care
You believe it anyway.

And there you go again
Reading my thoughts and memories.
There isn't much there,
It's bare
But you read them anyway.

Damon Naile

HAIL TO SPRING

Oh, how I've longed to see your face
Through all the dark and cold days.
And prayed that safely you'd survive
The harsh and cold winter days

Oh, Joy today I saw you stand
There in your lovely bridal gown
I knew that I would hold you soon
And you'd dispatch my wintry frown!

Marjorie B Dixon

CHOICE?

How easy it sounds to choose
Left or right?
Here or there?

Look closer
and see the dilemma -
to or fro?
Stay or go?

How much easier to remain
keep it all the same,
and yet hope,
for God's sake,
it changes.

A beautiful vacuum -
mountains and trees
and all the soul needs,
but no beating heart.

Change is a chance
to find Something,
Anything,
maybe, even
Me.

Christine Wilson

THE REASONS I LOVE YOU
(Dedicated to my wife Jeannie for all the happiness you've given me. Thank you. I love you. Always).

I love you for the way you sat down that night
As my heart overflowed with bottled-up emotion
And like a baby I cried a river of tears.
I love you for almost certainly saving my life
When I was so very close to ending it all
And you listened and gave me strength to go on.
I love you for falling in love with me
And showing me the true meaning of the word 'Love'
The happiness I found was truly fantastic.
I love you for the way my life has turned out
The hurt and despair, now love and affection
And those two things I never want to lose.
I love you for just being there for me
With loving arms and a heart of gold
And for loving me the way I want to be loved.
I love you for the belief you had in me
The achievements I've gained are proof of that
My poetry is inspired by you.
I love you for the marriage of our souls
United together, just you and me
And, although, during our life together
There maybe times I love you . . . more than I do
These are The Reasons I Love You.

Robin Grigsby

HOME TRUTHS

Wherever paths of life may lead,
   Whenever we should feel a need,
Whatever rights and wrongs we've done,
   Sweet thoughts of home warm like the sun.

I've travelled far, I've travelled wide,
   Like plankton on the restless tide,
Sought distant lands across the sea,
   Rejoicing in a spirit free.

Yet when I find the urge to roam,
   And stay in places, call them home,
I find there's no real substitute,
   The yearn for home becomes acute.

And even though I may surround
   Myself with good friends I have found,
The oldest and the best will be
   The ones back home awaiting me.

Each detail in my mind is bright,
   Each recollection brings delight,
Although so many years away,
   My dreams of home return each day.

Home brings a settled state of mind,
   With thoughts of loved ones, ever kind,
A place of rest, divorced from stress,
   Deep well of comfort in excess.

Glad thoughts of home we hold so dear,
   And cherish more each passing year,
Memories kept with tender care,
   A treasure house for us to share.

Geoffrey Elgar

The Old Railway

Mine is a single track
Watch how you go
A route well known
A tubular wisdom of tunnel vision
Trees a canopy
A wilderness overgrown
The trains have gone like solitary snakes
Caking mud covering their tracks
No stations left for people to wait

Others have taken their place
Bridges, platforms and complex tracks
Electric signals
Different routes for going there and back
Hustle bustle, tapping of heels
Network South Central humming along
Bleeping doors and silent wheels

Waiting on the deserted platform
Missed my chance yet again
To jump on the slow moving train
Tubular vision of it moving away
Its yellow back swallowed up
Now is nothing but an empty platform
And restless brain
The age of the train has come and will go
And I know that one day
This will be an old railway

Anna Moore

THE PATIENT PATIENT

Well, here we are son, in the Outpatients' Hall,
It is such a pity you had that bad fall.
Such a hustle and bustle, I never did see.
I hope Rose remembered to give dad his tea.

The nurses and sisters all look rather cross,
And the ambulance drivers still argue the toss.
Do we see a Mr or Dr today?
Their rank always muddles me in the affray.
If I get it wrong, they will just look like thunder.
Why are they always so touchy? I wonder.

The x-ray department is round to the right.
You'll soon be OK and we'll be home tonight.
Does your leg twinge? You look rather pale.
When the plaster is on you can tell them a tale
Your pals at the school will be signing their names.
And you will be longing to join in their games.
Never mind son. It could have been worse.
Oh! Look someone's coming. I think it's the nurse.

That white coated man was a doctor you saw.
He'd mistaken your name with that chaps fractured jaw.
The x-ray is taken. The plaster has set.
How many autographs do you think you will get?
The taxi is waiting. We won't be too long.
You know the old saying, 'Smile and a song.'

Just think of the poor souls we're leaving behind.
I do hope the doctors will be really kind.
So back to our semi, our warm cosy home,
And let us just pray you're not accident prone!

D Thorpe

DREAM TIME

My mum thinks I'm doing my homework,
with all that boring care,
but I'm galloping on a Palomino mare,
through a field, trees and all.
I'm on Space Mountain in Disneyland,
biggest ride there is, next Rickety Raft,
then my favourite, Diz.
I'm lunging a jet black stallion,
he's coming into me for a cuddle,
oh no the long reins got in a muddle.
I'm going to buy a hamster,
his colour, chocolate brown,
he's going round his wheel,
now he's running up and down.
That is my dream time over and done,
sorry . . . what were you saying mum?

Juliette Matthews (10)

THE OLD HORSE

The old horse stands in his field at rest
Dreaming of days gone by which were his best.
As a foal playing by his mother's side
When the world was new and his bones weren't tired.

People who had owned him over the years
Some good and kind, others he had feared.
He had tried his best to bend to man's will.
Didn't always understand what they wanted him to do.
Love and respect all he asked for in return.

Now on this bitter cold winter's day,
He shivers and moves closer to his companion, a large grey.
Together they stand by a thicket hedge
Which affords some shelter from the relentless wind.

He bows his head, eyes start to close.
Dreaming once again of a summer he will never see.
His days are numbered, soon no more to be.

Priscilla Winn

IN BED

Your deep dark eyes stare back at me
From a sea of bed linen
You don't speak but smile with your deep dark eyes.
I wonder how many women will see that smile
And fall under your spell?

I stretch out a hand to caress your soft silky skin,
And I am in love.
In love with every inch,
Every flaw,
Every nook and every cranny.

I want to run my hands
Over every inch of your skin
Keep you warm at night as it rains outside.
I want to feel your warm even breath on my cheek
As you sleep soundly by my side.

I am in love,
In love with you baby,
My son.

Elizabeth Hibbert

PORTLAND

In olden days, the tales are told,
Of men of daring, strong and bold.
The Portland folk lived on their Isle,
Survival meant hard work and guile.
Quarries of stone and flocks of sheep,
Pots of lobster, crab and such, to keep
Privation from these doughty folks door.

Severely blow the winds and tides,
Stealing husbands from their wives,
Leaving orphans and widows behind.
No welfare state to help them find
A living, or comfort in their need.
Life goes on, it must, indeed,
To keep the wolf from the door.

Wrecks of ships lie off our shores,
Their cargoes oft, without remorse,
Taken by the wrecking crews.
Goods to sell, or else to use.
Survivors ransomed for golden coin,
Or poorer folk, perhaps to join
The Islanders against their 'foe'.

Beacons lit, a clever plot,
Lured those ships on to the spot
To meet their doom on the ocean floor.
The excise men could do no more
But watch and hope to catch their prey
Sending them so far away
To return to England, never more.

Pirates used our rocky isle,
Hiding their spoils in deep defile,
Cave and tunnel, cellars deep.
Deeds more daring than tending sheep,
More exciting than catching fish.
Sons of masons would also wish
To join their peers in 'derring-do'.

Yarns of pirates and wreckers, bold,
Many a myth and legend told,
Preserve the Portland heritage.
Royal Manor, resist the change,
Refuse the trend to modernise,
A Weymouth suburb? Most unwise!
Remain an island, evermore!

Mamorald

Es

'Wheee!' Here we go in a kaleidoscope of colours,
Whirling round and round
On the helter skelter 'Es' going down and down
Roller-coaster, roller-coaster, up and down and round
A splurge of screams, nightmarish dreams, you have suddenly found
A bottomless funfair, the shies of coconut 'Es'
A dodgem's driving dream, until it comes to pay the fees
'Ha ha ha!' the clown does laugh as your money he does take
Distortion in the hall of mirrors
Where, sometimes you will wake
Other times the ghost train forgets
Your port of call
End of line, that's the time, to say
'Goodbye all.'

Kate Brown

Soul Growth

Imagine if you will the hairy caterpillar as he munches his way through leaf after leaf on the branch of a tree. Filling his little frame full of goodness to the best of his ability. When the allotted time span for his present existence is over he undergoes metamorphosis and changes into a chrysalis. To the onlooker it appears to be a form of hibernation, this is partly true, but, depending on how well the previous life has been nourished, will determine the transformation from caterpillar to chrysalis to beautiful butterfly.

Likewise you are in your caterpillar stage when you are young and learning all there is from the knowledge handed down from those who are around to guide you and from your own personal experiences. Your chrysalis time is when you put to good use all that you have been given and have gathered. For the service of mankind as a whole. Near and far. You are here to make a difference, to leave your mark, so to speak. Not for your own fame or notoriety. No, for the benefit of your fellow beings be they animal, vegetable or mineral. If you achieve fame along the way let it come from another's trumpet not yours. Then at the end of your earthly life, depending on how you have lived will determine how beautiful a butterfly you become in the next realm of existence.

Consider always that which was within you during your caterpillar stage is still within you and likewise so is all that was you during your chrysalis time. It is all part of the whole that makes you who and what you are today. Every day you gain in knowledge and experience. Use it wisely to the best of your ability and share with others all that is good and beneficial for them and your world. Thus you will be adding extra colour and brightness to your butterfly wings.

Dolly Little

THE GLOVE

But for the sun, where might we be but England?
With Georgian brick and well-raked gravel walks
Transported with the name, Hyde Park, to Sydney
As were the convict builders from the hulks.

Both in brown drab, two columns come ashore,
Approach the Hyde Park Superintendent's door.

The men, unfettered, still with minds in chains
And pale from close confinement, lacking health,
Now fearful, face constraints and future pains.
The rats, free immigrants, by stealth
Seek out by crevices and drains
To gain their secret commonwealth.

Alert to things mislaid that they might garner,
The ragman rodents ply by night in corners.

Discovered, with a century's elapse
Or more, from under floor is put on show
A fine lace glove, slipped from a lap perhaps
At dinner, and not found the board below.

Preserved by rats down deep in catacomb
Alike with convict wenches' linen caps,
Was some past theft of such slight prize the doom
Of her who laid the place or cleared the scraps?

Reluctant 'searcher' for this scrap of lace
Was it reminder of her fall from grace?
Did she repine for London
And the days when she was free,
As a ladies' maid,
Or to ply the trade
Of a Hyde Park jade,
In the shadow of Tyburn Tree?

G J Porter

The Emperor's New Clothes

The king of this land was very vain,
he loved all the best clothes so they say.
He cared not if sunshine or rain,
as long as he had new clothes every day.

Along came two swindlers who claimed to weave
the very best cloth which could not be seen
by anyone who was stupid or very naïve.
For to own this magical cloth the king was very keen.

He thought he'd be able to tell who was fit
to council the king in his state room.
The swindlers were paid in gold which they hid
and went to work on an empty loom.

The king sent his marshall to see the new cloth
but he was not going to be thought of as dim
and reported the work shone with gold gloss
and a richness in colour according to him.

The next one to see if progress was made,
was the chancellor and he said when asked,
the work was so good, he deemed it first rate.
The swindlers demanded more money to finish their task.

At last the king went to see for himself,
only to find there was nothing to see,
and not to appear stupid he looked on the shelf
and praised the wonderful cloth with glee.

At last the swindlers claimed the work done
and having been paid, sped on their way.
Meanwhile the king tried the new clothes on,
no one dared tell him he was naked all day.

But an innocent child called 'Look at the king!
He's as naked as naked can be,
in truth, he's not wearing a single thing.'
The people laughed, there was no suit for them to see.

H Lomas

EMBERS LEFT OF PASSION'S TIDE

A single droplet trickles down from the sea,
Pale face staring out
Distant voice screams to waves that don't hear
It's an ocean of lust you sink in the blood
As black ashes interfere with white sand
Sordid sea lets them join
The wind beckons on enticing to a paradise wreck
The waters rage with temptation
A temptress weeps on a raft
The wind lifts the ashes to the witch
They are   broken

The sand
Sinks
To
A
Depth
A bubble her fate as it claims that little grey soul.
Again she is trapped, a droplet
                    trickles
                    down
                        her stricken face
You see the ashes will remain in her heart.

Isobel Sangster

IT'S WHERE YOU FINISH

It isn't where you start
                It's where you finish
So, on that understanding
                Get cracking *now*
Make sure that what you *do*
                In the future
Is better than you've done before
                And how
You'll leave your mark whatever the cost
                No matter what your choice
Whether it be writing, or just your daily job
                Do it well
And you will have a voice,
                And make your mark whilst (living)
You'll be so glad in the end
                For it isn't
Where you start you see
                It's how you end
                        My friend!

Maisie Trussler

FUTURE JOURNEY

I would like to take a journey
Towards the distant stars:-
Perhaps, stopping for refreshments
On Jupiter or Mars.

The cost of this voyage
Will probably be high:-
What do you expect
For travel, through the sky?

There will have to be great progress,
In understanding time and space:-
An enormous leap in knowledge
For the human race.

I will not reserve my ticket
Until a future date:-
They only, take advance bookings,
For robots; charged:- As freight.

J Feld

THE FLOOD

The water washing at my feet,
The sun has sunk with the morning heat.
Birds hurriedly blown from beds,
Splashing, sinking, where are their heads?
Bread is bobbing and sinking fast.
Flapping, falling, I want to be last.
Animals struggling for big breaths of air,
The boisterous blows of wind, pushing my hair.
Stones not sinking due to wild worrying waves,
I have a good ghastly mind to go and hide in the caves.
The water waiting for banks to burst,
Banks might get better but this is the worst.
A mad rush racing through the woods,
Heads have been hidden in hooked up hoods.
It's racing with rain an umbrella is needed,
No-one's dressed up or wearing anything beaded.

Now it's time I said 'Goodbye'
Soon this flood should start to die.

Stacie Flood (11)

THAT TREE

That tree,
Stark and bare now before March winds,
Has stood there watching all my sixty years.
In rain and snow and sun
Its angular limbs and green-leafed shade
Have been a haven for the few and ordinary birds
Who've withstood their hedgerows brutal culling.
Today, as yesterday, it scans
The blue and distant Surrey hills
Which lift my heart each season
Highlighted by that tree.

That tree
No longer from its lean height
Views Italian POW's tilling the field below
Nor cows grazing, for grass lies fallow now,
As tonight, both to irritate and invite,
Benson's travelling fair roots itself
In an enclave on the field's untidy and puckered edge.

That tree,
Towering above nature and above time,
Has seen the ebb and flow of little suburban lives
So when tomorrow church bells ring
And the priest offers Christ's bread and wine for all
It will stand sentinel still
As residents of the street,
Like in previous barren yet affluent years,
Live in solitary splendour,
Like that tree.

Brian Frost

SHEBA

I had a dog called Sheba
She lived until she was 12
She had a full and contented life
I miss her being around
Her colour was a golden one, her eyes were shining brown
Her ears were floppy and always hanging down
She had her funny little ways
She would sit and speak for the ball
She'd run up the garden to collect them all
Back and forth she would go after each and every throw
I wish I could bring her back to see her once more
But I know that somewhere she is happy on a golden shore
If you see a shining star which seems to be with you wherever you are
I know it's sent from heaven above from Sheba to me with all her love.

P Hughes

COMPROMISE

Love's been here from the beginning of time
Learning to care is the bottom line
Together forever is what we all want
To share at all times is really the point

It's not a competition
There is no prize
The one word that works
Is compromise
So when there's a row
And you can't agree
Call on that word
And it will help
Just you see.

Linda Walker

MUM AND DAD DECEMBER 1998

A solitary moment
Frozen in time
Childhood memories
Such happy days of mine
Thank you for making those days so good
I can't live them again
But if I could I would
I never wanted to be
Anyone else but me
In those adolescent days
When I was young and free
it was great being Clare, Mum, Dad and me
This solitary moment, frozen in time
Is a constant reminder
Of many happy days of mine
It was all gone too soon
But it left me to see
That I never wanted to be
Anyone else but me.

Garry J Casalinie

LAWNMOWER SYMPHONY

Reluctantly the lawnmower is awoken from its dreamy sleep
Monday morning and every lawnmower is having grass for breakfast
Buzzing voices and whirling blades penetrate the spring stillness
Lawnmowers at ten o'clock
Smooth lawns take on a green baize appearance
Lawnmower symphony is now complete
It returns to the garden shed for a week's restful sleep

N Mason

LOVE HAS PASSED (THE ROBIN, NEVER)

The silence of you here is not
the pleasure of my heart.
Your sweetness now too far
to recall your sudden smile
by breezed rippled lakes we walked
our hand to feel
But now the trees have bent to wind
Our love the fallen leaves
and walk I on without a mind
to feel the winter's cold abyss
No comfort clothed me from the storm
Just stumbling without light to help
my weary soul pass through the darkness
of what seemed endless future time
And then one day the change it came
The robin sang its song
and this I called 'the nice.'
A multitude of other birds struck up as well
for my new found friend
They sang the chorus line
the words of which I can't recall
But something like it sounded
'You'll never walk alone'
we found, we knew a need to share
and for each other care
We also have a child now
be it a short-haired pussy cat
She is almost human though and loves our happy ways
And sir, well he just looks down and smiles
from the great divide
And us, that's what we call ourselves, will go on
The robin he'll come too.

Christopher Irwin Poynter

JEMIMA HOLLY'S BROLLY

Jemima Holly had a brolly
Red with yellow spots
It was her prized possession
Rain or shine she carried it everywhere
It was almost an obsession
One rainy, windy day
Jemima proudly raised it aloft
'See how it keeps me dry' she cried
Her companions sighed
'She is off again, puffed up with pride'
Suddenly a fierce gust of wind
Startled Jemima so, the brolly was let go
And it soared up into the sky
'Help me, help me, what can I do?'
Jemima was beside herself with grief
People rallied but what could they do
Over a large hedge it flew into a public park
There is the entrance, they all rushed through
A little old lady sat on a park seat
'Oh what a treat
Look what the sky has delivered to me
I'm soaked to the skin
But now look see a pretty brolly to protect me from the rain'
'Oh dearie why are you crying, are you in pain?'
Seeing Jemima by her side
'The brolly is mine,' she cried
The old lady looked sad
'I thought it was too good to be true'
Jemima impulsively said, 'Keep it, it is my gift to you'
At that moment the sun shone on the face of Jemima Holly without
                                                                                       her brolly

M Fowler

WHO, ME?

I looked round the room of old ladies again,
And remembered the other room, full of old men.
'So,' I murmured, 'Lord, what can I do?
They are wanted by no one, but so dear to You.'

'Is that my Margaret?' a feeble voice said,
Across the room in the corner bed.
'Oh, shut up,' said one at the end of the ward,
'Taint no use your prayin', there just aint no Gawd!'
But You heard.

She sat by the window, her sightless eyes closed,
Dreaming, perhaps of the day Ron proposed.
Their wedding . . . their children . . . their home
All now gone, but You saw Lord, didn't You?
And beside you, stood Ron.

You told me to do what I could, in Your name,
Just holding a hand, when the agony came.
The tears, and the loneliness, known only to You.
I'll comfort them, be Ron, and Margaret too
But help me dear Lord.

Words may not come in time of distress,
But love can be felt, in just a caress.
So give me the wisdom to feel each one's need,
Until you receive them, Lord,
Use me, indeed.

Joan E Edney

His Love Is So Great

O it would be such a terrible thing
If there were no little birds to sing.
We'd miss their colours, we'd miss their song,
We'd think that all the world had gone wrong.

Another calamity there would be,
If we could not find a leafy green tree.
Even in winter the evergreens stand,
Shedding their beauty over all the land.

Then what if the rivers had all run dry,
And no lovely white clouds up in the sky
What if the moon forgot to shine at night,
Robbing the world of its great light.

But God the creator of all these things,
Who also made us to laugh and to sing,
Would not allow all those things to be,
Because He loves us so much you see.

E Squire

Untitled

Don't listen to the thoughts
That go on inside your head
Spinning, swirling, round and round
Until you're cold and dead.

Don't listen to the discord
Like a song sung out of tune
You never will catch hold of it
It's like reaching for the moon.

Don't try to analyse yourself
It'll make you crazy if you try
If you think you're being honest
Then it's just one more damn lie.

Don't trust the thoughts inside your head
They'll play you false right from the start
Forget your thoughts, your eyes, your ears
And just listen to your heart.

L Fairclough

County Colours

The colours of a county, in many forms are seen,
Let us wander the lanes, fields and dells,
Springtime trees, flaunting shades of green,
Woodland winds playing among the bluebells,
Bright yellow daffodils, wave us on our way,
The white dainty snowdrop heralds a new day.

Some trees show silver among the gold and browns,
Their heads a riot of purple, red and pink,
Treasured mellow stone, seen in villages and towns,
Warm orange and gold sunset, seems to form a link,
The grey mist shrouds the top of the hills,
All around me it seems like a battle of wills.

Your county and mine, may look much the same,
To me, mine is special, and cannot be bought,
And each has its own claim to fame,
The treasures therein, are very much sought,
My Shropshire gives me tranquillity, joy and peace,
Treasures enough for me, until life shall cease.

D Garlick

BATHROOM SCALES - WEIGHT

I got on the bathroom scales; which was my first mistake
As the arrow went around to ten stone - not eight
I diet and diet as much as I can
But it still won't go to eight stone yet
So I've got to diet at a new intense rate.

I do my aerobics every day and try to watch what I eat
But no matter what I try to do the arrow still goes around to ten stone
                                                                every week
I don't know anything else I can do
Can anyone help me to lose weight, either, you or you

Three months have gone now and I am at last getting thinner
I'm only nine and a half stone now and feel like a winner
I now know that all it takes is to be patient
And feel pleased with yourself;
The weight will come off eventually if you only wait.

Anna P Aldridge

NIGHTMARY

She's a verinormous lady of substantial size,
Has a most voluptual bosom, and some mighty meaty thighs
Wears the biggest of goggles on the piggyest of eyes
And if ugly equalled wisdom, then, oh gosh, she would be wise.
And I really am quite glad she's not my mother

Her face looks quite like putty with a wobbleistic chin,
Her bulbous nose is mottled, and complete with bogie pin.
Exhibiting her tooth, she gives a gargoylistic grin.
If you found a face like this about, you'd put it in the bin.
And I really am quite glad, I'm not her brother.

Her shoulders, quasimodic, on a chap would look a treat,
And if knobbles are regarded, then her knees are hard to beat
Both her shoes are overflowing, they're so very full of feet.
You just wouldn't claim acquaintance if you met her in the street.
I really am quite glad she's not my lover.

Anthony D Parker

AS DRAWN BY LOWRY

Leaning into the shelter,
Seaspray across your face.
Grey, blue-silver, silver
You blend into the ocean's mystery.

Seagulls streak against the sky
Brilliant white on silver canvas.
A ragged dog pushes against the wind,
Then takes the slack.

In the distance a pencil man,
Arms up-stretched,
Chases across the beach,
Towards his tumbling hat.

A passing couple
Clasped together like walnut crackers
Double-shield against the wind.
A woman steps out

Of the artist's palette to
Greet the man in the shelter.
Gaily laughing, she skips and twirls
Oblivious to the angle of the wind.

Janet Bloomfield

TALKING FLOWERS

The flowers tell me all sorts of stories.
Starting in the spring with the snowdrop, she
Promises an end to hail, wind, rain and
Snow with the crocus, tulip and hyacinth telling
The same tale. When the summer comes, the
Peony, lily and iris tell of long, hot
Summer days with hours spent on the beach,
Raiding the cafes and restaurants and getting
Brown under the hot summer sun. The
Chrysanthemum tells of the plenty of autumn with
Fruit and veg ripening in the heat, filling our
Barns and storehouses for another winter. But
The best story of all is the story told by
The bunch of white roses Love carries as she
Parades the aisle on our wedding day, promising
Years of happiness, family, love and joy.

T Splitt

DAWNING

Stand with stillness on a quiet, calm morn.
Under beech, pine and oak, awaiting the dawn.
Watching a spider with thin silver thread
on dew-leafed branch, weave a fine web.
Echoing loud comes the trill of a bird.
Dawning is here and so are the herd
of deer from the forest.
Wraiths in the mist.
A sight to behold,
what more to be wished.

Patricia Bull

SUPERSTITION OR COMMON SENSE

The black cat
crossing your path,
You fall over it,
The black cat.

The leaning ladder,
You walk under it.
The paint falls.
The leaning ladder.

The falling picture.
You bend down,
Sore head.
The falling picture.

The howling dog,
dead of night
wakes you up,
The howling dog.

Superstition?
Common sense!

The cat - look down.
The ladder - look up.
The picture - look out!
The dog - look for his master!

May Cowan

The Taxman Cometh

Neighbours thought they were in the money
They were ringing out the bells
Thinking the taxman owned a fortune
They were gonny live like swells
Wife went down to Harrods
Posh shop in London toon
To buy up all their crinolines
And make the boys all swoon
She'll sit upon her chauffeur-driven
And wave to all her subjects
Hope she doesn't pick her nose, 'specially, in public
She's booked up for the love train
We hope she'll have success
But is hubby going with her, on the Orient Express?

Hubby's ordered a satellite dish
Jist tae waash his *heids*
A guitar, synth, stacker system
Are few of all his needs
They're gone tae hell in a barra
Everyone's jinin' in
They're throwin' wild night parties
An' swallyin' back the gin
They've given up their work too
Thinking they're big tycoons
Their street all shines in neon lights
lanterns and balloons
Hope they don't get a dissy
Fur *them* it'll no be funny
If the taxman calls an' says to them *'balls'*
It's you *that owe* us *the money*

E A Hutchison

MICE

If you get mice in your house it's not a nice thing,
They can eat a necklace or even a ring,
They will nibble your food,
Because they think that it's good,
Especially your cheese!

They can get in any way, even by the cat flap,
But there is a way to catch them, a trap!
You mustn't let it linger,
Or they might catch your finger,
And that wouldn't be very nice.

they make big holes in your wall,
To make it easier for them to crawl,
They can also make them on your door,
Or sometimes even on the floor,
And it makes your house look terrible.

So now you know the story of the mice,
You might start to think twice,
About where you keep your cheese,
Away from these little 'smees',
So remember, watch out for mice!

Siobhan Anderson (9)

HEAVEN

As I plunge deep, I feel my body revolving so neat,
I see blue alone, I feel cold shivers down my spine.

The speed is incredible, the sparkle is inevitable as the lights circle,
The movement is so perfect, beautiful, magical, peaceful.

What more could I ask for, heaven, this is like heaven.

Nicola Walker

Mankind's Madness

Man was given the greatest gift - life
Only to devise methods of taking it away
Why is it for mankind to understand nature,
He first has to destroy it?

We head now into the millennium.
The year two thousand awaits us.
Joyous scenes ahead you might think
Well, I for one am not looking forward to it.

We have placed man on the moon
Man-made structures orbit the earth
Yet, still millions of people are dying
Man was born free, politics enslaved him.

When will we get our priorities right?
We destroy nature and call it civilisation
Man was given the greatest gift - life
Only to devise methods of taking it away.

David Strauss Steer

Highland Deer

O mountains with your peaks of snow,
And heather with its purple glow,
You make me feel so much at home,
So on your mountain slopes I'll roam,
Water falling down the side,
Plenty to drink, much obliged,
I do not starve, lots to eat,
Very happy I must repeat,
From day to day I have no fear,
As I am a happy highland deer.

Alice Devita

LOCHGELLY

Three decades noo a've been wi' ye,
In this wee toon o' Lochgelly;
Afore a cam' a didna' ken
There wis a toon cried by that name!

It didna mean a thing tae me,
When first a heard o' Lochgelly;
A pictured it a beauty spot
Wi' trees an' lochs an' hills - the lot!

A pin-prick only on the map,
A day dreamt wi' it on ma lap,
An' whit a disillusionment
When first a saw this toon's content!

It seemed sae awful' wee and sma',
No' even a real toon a ta',
the loch's awa' richt oot the road,
An' humble the' av'rage abode!

But yince a got tae ken you folk,
A really liked Ye quite a lot;
An' efter a' the loch's real nice,
There's hills an' trees if Ye look twice!

A Cowan

A Stranger's Smile

Often
we feel forgotten,
unaware
all around us
walks unclaimed love.
Hungry hearts
looking for a stake,
a day to make.
So much giving to share
asking little in return.

I've found
that a perfect smile
from a glowing stranger
can be enough
to mend
the damage done
by
a thousand steely frowns.

Barry Cooper

Whoops!

I was given a vase some years back,
On moving some furniture, it went smack.
It was quite pretty and made me cross,
I was really sorry at the loss.

So keen to make it look like new,
I went out shopping to buy some glue.
Managing to fix the pieces in place,
It looked alright, but it leaked at the base.

Some time later my friend called,
She brought me some flowers, and was appalled
As her present to me fell apart,
I should have told her but I hadn't the heart.

Beulah Thompson

WALKING BACKWARDS IN ASDA

It is an ordinary day.
Women walk backwards in Asda,
and barricade passageways
vaguely with trolleys.
They wear jeans, designer-shrunk,
bleach-blotched, epidermal,
the better to display pudenda,
trendily to make much of little,
an ostentation of absence.

They read, re-read, and read again
the labels on the tins of beans,
fight their corner at the cashier's desk,
and queue, reluctant to relinquish
the cosy terror found within,
to brave the unknown terror out.

It is an ordinary day.
Women walk backwards in Asda,
and Safeway, and Finefare,
and Tesco, and Presto, and Spar,
and in Boots The Chemist.

W Oliphant

TAKING THE BISCUIT!

Now, we Scots just *love* our biscuits
by they chocolate (pearl!) or plain.
Our hands are eager, stretching out
when the plate comes round again.
We watch it on its endless way
as each biscuit is 'picked-off' -
the one you've got *your* eye upon
someone will surely scoff!
But, when at home, and by yourself
with a new, unopened tin,
no need to hurry, take your time,
drool over the display within.
And, as you ponder, weigh each up,
(and disregard impending pounds!)
you sample one, then - just one more -
your greed, alas, just knows no bounds!
You're then so full, no room for tea -
why *did* you cook substantial stew? -
you laugh, and say you're *dieting*
(well, it's, almost, sort-of, true!)
And when to bed at last you go,
you wake up in the night -
you're feeling hungry - what to do? -
you really feel you need a bite!
You try to sleep, shut fast your eyes -
tantalising images appear
of *biscuit tins,* that *beckon* -
but - mind - avoid that *creaking* stair!

Joyce Hockley

SPRING HAS SPRUNG

The winter days were long,
I was feeling really low,
I longed for warmer days
And the sun to make me glow.

Then suddenly it came
Like a spirit in the night
Spring had sprung like magic,
And now the world looked bright.

Looking from my garden,
I saw a cloudless sky,
The sun warmed my body,
I waved my blues, goodbye.

A blackbird on the apple tree,
Announced it with his song,
And all around I found the clues,
That proved he wasn't wrong.

There was a bud, a shoot, a flower,
All anxious to appear,
I was so overcome,
I shed a little tear.

And so I stood in reverence,
I said a little prayer,
And thanked God my Creator,
For the beauty everywhere.

Margaret Findlay

INCREDIBLY ALONE TODAY

Incredibly alone today . . .
Whilst the sun shines bright
And in my sight the blue sea ripples on the shore,
But here no more are you.

No one knows just where I am.
Not a single soul in this whole world
Knows I'm sitting here with this awful fear
Of being alone.

I wish that figure down on the beach
Was you, strolling barefoot in the sand.
I would run and take your hand
And we would walk for miles as we once did,
With smiles, and the feeling that
Together we were not alone.

Oh, why does the sunshine make me cry?
Why does it have to be
That I can't see the world without seeing you?
When all in life is new again
And I am so aware that you're not there
To share this world with me.

And yet, the birds still sing,
The daisies bloom, and yes, there's room
In my heart to feel the sun,
And know I'm not just one alone,
But you are here . . . somewhere, somehow . . .
In every ray of sun, in every breeze,
In the ripples of the waves.
And that figure on the shore . . .
Well . . . maybe it *was* you . . .

Anne Beattie

GRANDMA IS GONE

Grandma is gone
Never did I think I would have to believe those words

For you gave me so much love
You cared for me since I was born
You know how much I love you
And wish you were here today
But there is something I need to tell you
We all love you dearly, in our own special way

I love you so much
And I am grateful for your love in return
We all shall mourn for you today
Because you have shared a special part in so many people's lives

You always seemed to put others before yourself
You gave so much
And now you are gone
Today we are here to say goodbye
But death is not the end
It is the beginning of a new life

We all know you are in God's loving care
We have to learn to leave you there
Where life is peaceful and free from pain

We shall mourn with sadness in our hearts
And you will remain with us through
Until we meet again

To grandma with all my love.

Cassandra Simms-Sawyers

BEDTIME STORY

Come sit on my knee, my little one
It's story time once more
Let's cuddle up beside the fire
There is a wonderland in store
Quiet as a little mouse
You wait expectantly
You love your bedtime story
Your little face so bright with glee
The story book you bring to me
I know which story it will be
Each story you know off by heart
So come my love we'll make a start
Then I begin, you'll interrupt
This happens every night
I'll let you tell the story
Although it's not quite right.

Edwina Ainscough

A LOG CABIN

A large log cabin beside a shining lake
Rocking chairs on the porch what a picture it would make
A hammock swaying gently in the summer breeze
Half surrounded by great tall trees
A garden at the side full of vegetables, fruit and flowers
For me to work during daylight hours
Sitting on the porch in the evening shade
Gazing at the wonders that nature has made
Cat and dog lying at my feet
I think that kind of life would be rather neat.

J M Peek

CHRISTMAS

A sparkling shining, purple ball
holds me, trance-like, holds my all
though I am small, it makes me tall
as fur lined branches dance then fall
dancing in this sea of green
outstretched limbs evergreen
tinsel tipped branches bend
with parcels, messages to send
reindeers sledging into night
I lie awake, watch the light
as in the twinkling of your eye
all childhood dreams satisfied.

Now this season has returned
all misty eyed and over-runned
the globes return upon the tree
and in their mirror, still, is me
in the ticking of the clock
as it draws to twelve o'clock
expectation is now gone
of miracle births with the dawn
instead it's me and there it's you
and there's a place somewhere for two.

J Mulholland

WHEN THE RAINS CAME

Rivers of water torrenting down
from the back-lying hills,
rushing over drains protesting
their inadequacy to cope.
Crudely constructed walls of
sandbags giving some hope
to folk in the swamped valleys
where stands their home.

Well done! Well done, they've
changed the flow
directing it to the field where
moss and rushes grow:
where once the games of youth
were played;
where now, alas, young girls get laid
and vandals roam.

Climatologists, no Mystic Megs or
Cassandras these scientists who
predict more rain; more rain in
northern parts and drought elsewhere.
Less sun, says they, and yet
the ice-caps melt away, sea-levels rise;
it's no surprise the ozone layer is
worn away by overuse of aerosol spray
and suchlike things that smell quite nice,
and at the same time, melt the ice.

In future years, where islands were
the foaming surge of windswept waves
destroys the last remains that humans
built; and yet the guilt of avarice
continues unrestrained -
cosmetics, used by the vain,
profane in their quest for beauty:
and damn the ice!

Whatever more the future holds for
we who claim superior intellectual powers
o'er all Earth's beings.
Yet, animals of the field and forest
know that changing weather patterns
deplete their numbers - while man,
profligate in all things, continues
on the path of planet Earth's destruction!

George Findlay

MEMORIES OF SUMMER

The song of the blackbird,
The smell of the dew,
In summer these are but a few!

The smell of the flowers after the rain
The buzz of the bees, the sting of the pain!
Young green trees, swaying in the breeze,
Just lazing around, doing as we please.

Happy laughter of the children,
Looking so brown,
Summer dresses, while going to town,
Strawberries and cream and nice cool lollies
Just for now, forgetting about brollies!

Off from school for such a long time
Enjoying the freedom, oh so divine.
Getting up early, staying up late,
Catching the daylight before it's too late.

When autumn arrives, such happy memories
Of these long hot days, and summer revelries.

Ann Stevenson

THE ICE-CREAM

I stood at the gate by my granny's cottage,
mid summer heat shimmered on the tar,
the bend ahead shaded from sun long due.

I stood waiting as I do each Sunday for the sound,
the tinkle of bells sharp and clear, I wait so long to hear.

The shilling in my sweaty palm, so shiny and round,
soon it will be transformed into the best thing all week,
cool white as snow on a hot, hot day.

Piled so high on a cone of gold, this ice-cream is a thing to behold,
I pay the man and lick my lips as it's made,
I reach so high as he hands it down, see you next week, enjoy.

I turn to face the gate, to eat it in the shade of the apple tree,
slowly walking towards me wearing a large straw hat,
her strawberry hat she called it when she picked.

Her hands red from the juice, reached out with terrifying slowness,
I have not tasted one of those in years, may I try?

As if powerless to stop myself, I held out my hand,
all week I waited for this beautiful treat,
why did I not go home, it was only a few yards.

Then the mouth opened, the tongue slowly came out,
and seemed to take for ages to finish the lick,

My cone was destroyed, the magic was gone,
oh how nice she said.

When she bent to pick the red berries,
I dumped it behind the tree.

Slowly walked home as if I had just lost a friend,
so sad, I could not share, my precious cream.

James Cartmell

BIG BROTHER

Once we shared a room,
now we share a wall.
He was always there to catch me
should I ever fall.
When I had a nightmare,
I'd creep in through the door.
'Can I come in?' I'd ask.
'Sure, what are big brothers for?'

I'm not sure when it happened.
I'm not sure when it came.
He started to grow up,
but I just stayed the same.
I didn't see it coming,
then all of a sudden I saw.
Somehow he had changed,
he's not just my brother anymore.

Perhaps there are too many years between us.
Perhaps there are too few.
But years after he'd grown up,
I began to grow up too.
And now it's he who doesn't realise.
It's he who doesn't see.
I'm not only his little sister anymore
Now, I'm also me.

Gemma Cole

A Dream

I have a dream of fame and fortune
I have a dream of love and peace
Sometimes I dream that I can fly
Way up high in the clear blue sky
With fresh wind upon my face
Away from war and the human race
Then in the cool light of the day
My dreams all fade away
Back to reality, back to the ground
Back to the troubles all around
Drugs, violence, war and hate
You never know what's outside your gate
What can we do to make things good?
How can we get ourselves understood?
Will there be less people unemployed
Or will the world be destroyed?
All the answers we will never know
So we will continue to go with the flow
And just continue to dream our dreams
And maybe one day they won't *be just dreams.*

Grace Brown

All The Roofs Of London

Above the choke and cloaking city on a winter's morning clear,
Two stand, cold scratched hands before an open sky.
High upon the frost brushed hill, you and I,
Consider what we hold most dear,
The view below or the one so near.
I know full well, as I turn from body to city that lies,
While with excited breath, a mist that freezes on your lips you cry,
'I can see all the roofs of London from here.'

On elevated green rising with the day,
The weak, new born sunlight shines on,
Laughter lines around your face.
Rhythmic throb of tube train spear, spiralling away,
And all the roofs of London,
Bow down to us in grace.

Ian Dixon

THE NURSE

The angels with their gentle hands
Are always there on station,
So tenderly they care for us
With the utmost dedication.

> Docs do their operations
> Then to the side they stand,
> And leave the care of patients
> In the nurses' careful hands.

Most patients treat them with respect
But the odd one shows disdain,
Though all agree they're always there
To help us through our pain.

> They are always there or thereabouts
> Through long days and lonely nights,
> When I press that little buzzer
> Someone's quickly by my side.

Oh I feel so very humble
As I pen this little verse,
For in hospital what would we do
Without our friend, the nurse.

The Portonian

DALMATIAN

I love Dalmatians
they're soft as brushes
bouncing around
like something gone mad.

I love Dalmatians
they run fast as Linford Christie
leaping and jumping
getting all the attention.

I love Dalmatians
soft and cuddly
falling asleep upon your knee.

Aimee Upton (13)

MOTHER'S DAY

Looking on,
I see you in the
Way that I am.

Angel that you are,
Your love is a wave
Washing over me:
Always there and
Never to run dry.

Angel that you are,
Know what you are
And smile.

E V Salmon

LACOCK IN SUMMER

The day dawned sunny, off we went
Had brunch, then on our way
To Lacock village, through its street
To Abbey, saw on way.

Fox Talbot's pictures, Abbey rooms
Some large, and some quite small
Then, into cloisters cool and still
Returning to main hall.

Then, out into the sunshine
Past lawns so fresh and green
Next, into village tea-room
So restful, bright and clean.

Took time to sit, and to enjoy
Refreshing pot of tea.
Then on to gift shop and the church
Flower festival to see.

Time now for homeward journey
And to think back once again
Of the sights we'd seen in sunshine
And not a drop of rain!

Doris Cowie

Why?

Before you shoot me or rape my wife
Spare my children's precious little lives
I don't understand the reason or cause
Man's inhumanity to man is not of any god's laws

Is it in the name of religion you kill, torture and maim?
Is it the politics that you do this with no hint of shame?
Is it the greed for power and wealth?
Or is it the murderous lust for your egotistic self?

Before you pull the trigger just tell me why
Does raping one's wife justify your cause's cry
In murdering my children who committed no human crime
Or wrecking my home in this holocostic time?

If you're not barbarian put away your guns
Fight your fight in a peaceful way, do not slay my sons
Put your arms around my wife give her a friendly hug
Are you sane and gentle or an armed and dangerous thug?

Ian McFarlane

Eden

Eve said to Adam
Go on take a bite
I'll take one just to show you
That everything's alright.

They bit, they chewed,
They spat out the seeds,
And then they knew
The gravity of their deeds.

Now Adam is down
And with a sadness he sighs,
Eve shouldn't have listened
To the serpent's slithery bribes.

But Eve is quite happy
To know wrong from right,
And with a keen smile
She takes another bite.

Maureen Cropley

First Flight

They told me 'You'll love flying'
There's really nothing to it!
Like sitting on a bus my dear,
So safe, you'll always do it.
They told me about duty frees
And in-flight meals and drinks,
They told me airlines span the globe,
And how the whole world shrinks,
But nobody told me there are mountains in the sky,
With peaks of solid silver, so bright they hurt the eye,
And nobody told me there are canyons everywhere,
With banks of golden roses and walls of angel hair,
And nobody told me, as you fly from day to night,
Of the miracle of colours
As the sun drops out of sight,
If only they had told me it was beautiful and bright
I could have experienced years ago
The thrill of my *first flight!*

P Bates

GOD'S MISSING BIT

God was sitting looking puzzled,
He had lost a piece of heaven,
Looking down upon the world,
He could see it had landed in Devon.

Rolling hills, valleys so green,
The granite spectral tors,
Oceans of blue, rivers running,
And the awesome vastness of the moors.

The cathedral city of Exeter,
Crowds bustling to and fro,
With all Devon's beautiful features,
Numerous choices of where to go.

Historic places of interest,
Unending tales of ghosts,
Packed with mysteries all over,
Stretching from moor to coast.

To spoil such beauty would be a sin,
Let us marvel at the sight,
We will not let God have it back,
It's ours now, by his given right.

Glennis Horne

Too Late

As trees fall with soft sighs
And seas become a silty sludge
Whilst thickened air stings the eyes
Too late a conscience starts to nudge
But still a prey of greed and lies
Cannot concede we did misjudge
As all the beauty quietly dies

As all the beauty quietly dies
We all bow down to progress
And watch the oil rigs rise
What's a forest more or less
Look at what the money buys

Lift up our hands to grab the gold
Given to us for what we've sold
Though never ours to sell
Hold high the cup of avarice
As we settle down to hell

To your child the sulphur dawn
Of a barren future morn
When a mutant apparition
Asks of the one which gave it birth
Bleary eyed and wetly drooling
'What was a thing called Earth?'

Jill Reeve

THE MEDIA

So let not your poison spread
That we digest in daily doses
And through your poison print
The devil and you proposes.

The lives and loves of the so-called famous
From you to us relate
The beautiful, the bad and the ugly
You serve us on a plate.

These folk of low morals
Their ego leaves us cold
Models and comic singers
A brass neck that makes them bold.

The weirdoes on the catwalk
With their so-called beauty
The sick and sullen faces
With eyes jet-black and sooty.

The sound of disco music
Gaudy lights that offend the eyes
Ghetto blasting music
And the dancers getting high.

The noisy, screeching voices
Of the so-called pop singers
It's nigh on forty years
The noise, still it lingers.

Some may call this paranoia
And maybe, they could be right
Is it me that's getting older
Or have I seen the light.

J McElroy

THOUGHTS OF AN OLDER WOMAN

What does it mean
To be seventy odd?
Where I did run
Do I now plod?

Where go the years?
And what do I learn?
To accept things as they are
And no longer yearn?

Never I say, thoughts are
As vibrant as yesterday.
Hopes undiminished
So much unfinished.

Precious years now
For the why and the how
To reach out
With love and compassion.

And so confound fashion
That says I'm not seen.
What do 'they' mean?
Perhaps I should scream.

No doubt I acclaim
Seventy odd is all gain.

Constance Wateridge

A TWIN AND MOTHER OF TWINS

We have spend every day
twinned as brother and sister at birth,
enjoyed each other's company
as we played.

Now the beauty of you, as sister,
and mother of young Robert,
you create the twins of your own
that we both were and have been.

We both had the same room
and faced each other as we slept,
we touched our tongues for a laugh -
to see what adults did!

When we grew and had separate rooms
we swapped the rules of:
'Come to your door'
for a late night chat!

The incredible thing is that
your twins are two little boys;
Patrick and Matthew.
But like us, they are new people
and very different little ones.

They look at your face and smile
and you see part of yourself within them.
They are part of you -
and you are part of them.

They will help you remember the days
when you, yourself, were that age.
The games they play together
and the humour they entertain
will remind you exactly
what a twin will always have.
Their other half.

They love you as their 'mum'
and I love you and thank you
for being
my twin sister and my friend.

Declan O'Sullivan

SAD DESECRATION OF AN ISLAND ROUNDABOUT

Who took away the chestnut trees
That stood on an island fair,
Those beautiful trees for all to please
Which, alas, are no longer there?

Where, oh where, is our little island,
The gateway to Hucclecote and Glos,
With the daffodils ringing the chestnut trees
That graced the island's charm?

Gone, gone forever, like an act of theft!
My pulse quickens as I simmer in my anger,
And to see there's nothing left,
But bulldozers, hydraulics and danger.

Farewell, little island and charming trees,
Where birds once gathered on your boughs,
And where tall grasses swayed in the breeze,
Amid all seasons you flowered with ease.

Now my lungs burst asunder with foul fumes
Now more than ever before.
Man curses planet like a mad predator,
And despoils all that he should applaud.

George W Lansbury

NONA

What goes up, must come down
Two and six were half a crown
You will drive me around the bend
I'll stick it out to the bitter end
He's worth his weight in gold
She's too slow to catch a cold
Leave it alone, I'll do the rest
Is that what you call your best?
It's greener on the other side
I'll say this with great pride
They say it's darkest before the storm
Bird will sing at break of dawn
How many times are these things told?
Not just once, more like ten fold
In what strange age did these sayings start?
Are we English worlds apart?
You can bet your bottom dollar
They will go on and on.
Is that why things are often written
By someone called Anon?

M J Boden

GRANDMA'S GERANIUMS

Geraniums like Grandma used to grow
Towering tall upon window sill
How she used to love them
Fond memories I have of them still.

Now I too grow geraniums
Water, then watch them daily grow
I think of my dear Grandma
Oh how she loved hers too.

What is it about geraniums
In fashion they are all the time
Out in garden, in tubs on patio
They all look so refined.

It's you, Grandma's geraniums
So tough, yet bright to cheer
You never let us down at all
A little water, and you flower all year.

J Cook

A FAR AWAY DREAM

There once was a girl called Emily,
She loved to go on holiday.
Cash was short you see,
And this wish was a long way away.
By night and day she prayed.
Mum was sad she could not oblige,
And around Emily her arm she laid.
The brochures she eyed from page to page,
Then one day Mum said
'I have a surprise.'
Emily sat with dread.
Then the light shone in her eyes as Mum said
'I've won some money at bingo,
So darling Emily on holiday we can now go!'
Away went Emily's woe,
She gave a cheer,
And wiped away a tender tear,
Her dream come true is here.

J Darts

URBAN EXPANSION

The North Avon Region of England
has expanded tremendously,
it is now South Gloucestershire
- a somewhat large county -
incorporating: Industry, housing estates, schools,
supermarkets, sports centres with swimming pools,
hospitals, libraries, zoos, night-clubs,
seaside resorts, 'theme parks' and pubs!
Manor houses, which are very grand,
some have wild animals on their land;
visitors pay to tour around those places,
contributing towards the upkeep for: 'Their graces'!
Fortunately, some 'green belt' still remains,
however, transportation is horrendous
and there is need to modernise the trains . . .
A metro-system beneath the ground,
might relieve pollution, congestion and sound;
perhaps an offer of shares for residents in the UK,
would cover the cost and massive outlay?
Everyone could benefit from the scheme,
which would also fulfil 'the conservationists' dream!
A sensible balance could be achieved,
by commuters travelling above and beneath;
people would find it easier to breath,
such as: Asthma sufferers and 'the hayfever prone',
who would be less likely to sneeze
and we could all participate in planting some trees . . .

D A Spence-Crawford

THE VILLAGE GREEN

Sitting on the village green
On a sunny afternoon.
I can hear the organ playing
For a wedding to be here soon.

It really is a lovely church
With pretty railings around.
I hope the marriage will be happy
And true love they have found.

I'm sitting here reminiscing
Of the days that used to be.
When the vicarage across the way
Held fetes and things and teas.

The chestnut trees are beautiful
The grass all mown and neat.
It has seen a lot of people
And lots of tiny feet.

Children going from school to church
On special occasion days.
I'm glad the school is doing well
One of the best, they say.

The shops that nestled around the green
Have gone, it's such a shame.
They sold stamps, and food and clothing
Almost anything you could name.

Well I must get going
Back to another life.
The old days come back so easily
When there was peace, not strife.

Winifred Shore

For All Of Your Life

The first thing in life for all to know,
Is the way to behave wherever you go,
For it's this that is seen by all that you greet,
When you shake the hand of people you meet.

Your eyes say as much as the sound of your voice,
They are given to you and not by your choice,
The twinkle that comes from the thought in the mind,
Has been with us all since the start of mankind.

Body language is also another concern,
It is seen by all wherever you turn,
The shake of the head needs no sound of your voice,
But is sometimes regarded as not being so nice.

Speak for yourself and hold nothing inside,
It will always be seen as part of your pride,
The truth therefore must be your number one,
You will then rest contented when the day's work is done.

Hopeful over years of a very long life,
To share it with a loving husband or wife,
So thank the Lord for what's been given to you,
Just always enjoy whatever you do.

__Gerald Marsh__

THE OUTSIDE CAT

From my window I can see
The outside cat, sitting under a tree.
She wears a plastic collar, sleeps in the grass -
Food delivered - sometimes - on an old plate.

Why did you take her
If you didn't want her?
No warm hearth, curled up by the fire
Like my lot, sleeping in the warmth all day;
No lap to sit on, no strokes or play,
Except a passer-by, occasionally . . .

The outside cat is nameless,
Her collar serving no purpose
But to rub the fur from her thin neck;
Just skin and bone and soft black fur . . .

Surreptitiously at night,
I creep out to offer her a saucer of cat food . . .
She looks round nervously,
Takes a few bites, just a few,
But her stomach is now too small
To take any more.

Just enough to survive on
That's all she's used to.
And I, too lax, too lazy,
Too busy with my own life,
To speak to the owner, do anything more,
Am also to blame.
So the outside cat continues to live under the tree,
To live out her life never knowing
How different it could be . . .

D Price

LITTLE MISS HOWARD

Everyone tells me that I have dainty feet.
Uncle Norfolk once told me they'll dance me to court.
He's really quite nice, he gives me kindly advice; he says
'Tread lightly my sprat let's see who you'll catch!'

>   *Step Pretty-O. Hop Pretty-O.*
>   *Who'll be my love!*

Everyone says I have adorable eyes.
Aunt Agnes once said they are my very best asset.
In corridors, in passing, she sheds other pearls of wisdom
'Poor girls need looks, and a bed for good luck!'

>   *Step Pretty-O. Hop Pretty-O.*
>   *Who'll be my love!*

All the men have noticed I have perky pert breasts.
The king tries to touch them, when he gets near me.
He whispers of innocence, his need for a queen.
He's writing me a poem about a lion and a doe.

>   *Step pretty-o. Hop pretty-o.*
>   *Who'll be my love!*

Both Gilbert and Rodney love my thin legs.
They praise my soft thighs, with their hands in my skirts.
I'm lucky, I know, to get such attentions.
Lucky that life has given me admirers.

>   *Step pretty-o. Hop pretty-o.*
>   *Who'll be my love!*

But you know, no one ever praises my luvvily long neck.
I only hear it mentioned when I am dancing.
I hear it in the twitterings, the rude wagglings of tongues.
Won't anyone tell me what they say about my neck?

> *Step pretty-o. Hop pretty-o.*
> *Who'll be my love!*

Gavin Stewart

THE GRANDMOTHER CLOCK

Where has the grandmother clock gone to Mummy dear?
Grandma left it to me in her will so she did.
I liked to watch it tick-tocking away.
It stood out like some great medieval momento,
but then it strayed from the mantelpiece to the
hall on its way to the threshold of home and has
now curiously disappeared altogether.
I used to peer at its mechanism and snigger at
its observing of our family gatherings as if
watchdogged and glued to the wall.
It shone like a chrysalis. A cocoon immemorial.
A beacon at night. Don't meddle.
It saw some sights. Frilly nighties.
Lace bodices. Pyjama games.
Warm and inviting. A geared timepiece collective.
Funny old watcher. Grim reaper kept at bay until
doomsday comes. The grandmother clock smothers
us in swaddling clothes. You cannot deny her.
She smiles gracefully. Teaser. Mother's keeper.
Snug calendar's mate. Home defender.
Time creeps by.

David Whitworth

MRS BRONSMOOR

She's on her own, her husband died.
He had an illness, then he died at home.
Had a bad night, the doctor came and said
We shouldn't move him, it would cause distress.
I'll send a nurse. But then within an hour he died.
So now she carries on.

You see her pass, she's walking.
She never learned to drive.
Besides, to run a car costs money
And she can afford a bus.

She carries on, she visits more
She stays a little longer, now no need to hurry home.
The pattern's still the same.
Perhaps she's quieter, not so up-and-down.
Does she think less or more?

She carries on, for when you're old that is the easy thing
To change would mean to think again
Quite hard, and plan a life once more.
And so, she carries on.

R Tapley

MARTEG BRIDGE

Steep majestic mountains
Against the deep blue sky
Sheep wander on the slopes
And rabbits scamper by.

Close by, the river flows
The foaming waters splash
Tossing over boulders
Canoeists leap and dash.

Foxgloves stand so proudly
Bees buzz in the heather
Short tormentil growing
In the summer weather.

On frigid days its bleak
Feet crunch the frozen snow
The mountains look like Alps
The wind, a bitter blow.

Wendy Dedicott

HEREFORD CIDER

Meg is her name, she's broad in the beam
But don't underestimate her.
Her stockings are sheer, bold black they gleam
And she's gingham wrapped up in fur.

Simple and shy yet the gleam in her eye
Warns well the Meg is not simple.
Take her for a drink and ere you say 'Goodbye'
'Twill be plain as can be that you tipple!

Sit down with your Meg turn your back on the keg
You feel big and strong and hearty.
She'll string you along till her favours you beg
And you're life and soul of the party!

Too soon you must go and from Meg depart.
Time with her is pleasant and sweet
You stand upright feeling you've lost your heart
And fall in a heap at her feet.

Ruth Mollon

On Holiday But Missing Home

As I read this book of prose, I think about myself and those
I who holiday afar, to my dad t'would seem a star
'A Shropshire Lad' is called the book
My father of't would take a look
In the book's image was he cast
A Shropshire lad but times go fast
As in the church yard laid at last
So lie amongst his Shropshire soil
No more for him life's work and toil
And often when I wonder why
He had to die to reach the sky
When for myself in mighty jet the sky is mine
And sun will set upon another land tonight.
In Spain the tavern lights are bright
But as dusk falls the brandy glass
On a strange balcony alas.
I'm nothing but a country lad
Shropshire's for me just like my dad.
I'll holiday on foreign soil but deep inside me it would spoil
My happiness for evermore, in death laid on a stranger's shore
And like the poet in far town signing as to his rest laid down
Thinking of Shropshire's hills and plains
I simply smile and hide my pains
To home I shall return at last
Shropshire's my home while time shall last.

C Growcott

BRISTOL
(An infamous past)

Bristol was just one point on a triangle of torrid despair
Seventeenth century produced goods founded its prosperity.
Cargo shipped from the docks to West Africa and traded for slaves
Previously kidnapped or captured in inter-tribal warring.
Shackled, they were forcefully marched to the coast and
                                                     pushed into ships
Scant food, filth, poor sanitation and disease led to many deaths
On the Middle Passage to America or the Caribbean.
Paraded and examined like cattle, overlooked by buyers
For the harsh plantation owners, the fittest were always picked first.
Cotton, sugar, cocoa, coffee, tobacco back breakingly grown.

Later exported here to be refined, processed and then sold on
Thus merchants' wealth gave employment to numerous local people
From outgoing alcohol, textiles, blue glass, metalware and guns.
The past cannot be changed and still misunderstood by some today.
Progress is looking forward to fight injustice for all in need.
The newly constructed horned bridge spans and links
                                           the cobbled dockside.
Aptly named Pero Bridge after a black manservant to gentry
The Pinney family who lived in elegant Georgian splendour
From profitable sugar plantations owned on Nevis Island.
Past horrors for future generations finally put to rest.

M E Beale

WHISPER

Whisper in the stars
echo in the sparks
resounds through the scars
and that amazing sound
drifted in the deluge of blue
without any clue
is somehow too loud.
Maybe cos the confusion of words
uttered by the quiet voice
offering gently the choice
in the frontiers of space
completely untouched and mysterious
that sound without the face
innocent but mischievous.
Whisper floats able to cope
with the altitude of the waves
dancing in the bluish slope.
Whisper so crazy in its pride
some days noisy and very bright
for the rest quiet and heavily light . . .
Tries to make a gain
again and again
looking for the magic words
which only one in the universe knows
and for us they sound plain
without the infinite pain
hidden in the truth of states . . .
Can you hear? . . . the echo germinates . . .

Jolana Hoskova

THE WHITE FLOWER

A single white flower was left on the floor,
When the funeral cortege slowly trailed through the door,
Altar candles still flickered, wisps of smoke in the air,
An old lady stood quietly, a black veil on her hair.

As the last of the friends made their exit from church,
An owl blinked an eye, his claws clung to their perch,
He lived in a hole, in an oak, by the gate,
Folks could see him at night, if passing by, very late.

The vicar led mourners up the path to the grave,
Her crocodile flock was just like a wave,
Family members were crying, and blowing their noses,
The small coffin was covered in carnations and roses.

Inside the church, hymn books were collected,
Donations added up, the deceased was loved and respected,
Muffled bells tolled their message up above in the tower,
The old lady saw white petals from a beautiful flower.

The church was soon tidied, the candles blown out,
All pews quickly checked - no belongings left about,
The old lady saw rays of very bright light
Beaming through coloured windows to the flower so white.

She picked up the petals, fragile, innocent and pure,
They came from a rose, of that she was sure,
A young girl had died and was buried this day,
The flower, its petals, had withered away.

Anita E Matthews

OLD JACK

Old Jack knows his time is nearly up.
It's not that he even cares too much,
'cos life ain't been very kind to him, see,
and it sorta plays havoc on the poor old bones
when yer got no place to call home.

No kip to be got on a cold, toilet floor,
with cloth-wrapped feet poked out under door.
Ok when it's raining, but them folk keep complaining:
Them ones rushing by, with scorn in their eyes,
when yer plead for a penny or so.
Bet they don't thank God they're able to go
scurrying on to the warmth of their homes.

He whiles away the hours, counting pigeons in the park,
hunched up in an over-sized mac and grey woollen hat.
And he don't give a toss 'bout the rain beating down,
trickling cold and wet down his back.
He takes a swig of stout and keeps right on swigging.
And he don't give a toss 'bout his gummy grin
as the blurred sea of faces swims by,
just lifts an arm in a shaky salute,
but he's blowed if he sees them smile.

So he soldiers on toward a nearby tree,
pain aplenty piercing his chest,
but his legs give way, and his head comes to rest
on a bed of sodden leaves;
and hail hammers down on his wrinkled brow,
but so what, anyhow?
For old Jack knows he's not long to go;
there's nothing can harm him now.

E Henley

HOLIDAY IN EXMOUTH

I feel like a gypsy in this big caravan
So I start to imagine places in far away lands
I know it would be so easy to roam
If I had to make this caravan into my home
But the trouble with caravans is you hear every noise
Folks watching television, children playing with toys
Every footstep feels like an earthquake's begun
But I have to admit it is lots of fun.

In today's caravans it's like home from home
Not like the caravans of years long ago
Hot running water, a shower or bath
In my old caravan, don't make me laugh
Soft padded seats, carpets on the floor
Even three bedrooms and all have doors
A kitchen so well equipped it could make you sigh
In fact it's nearly as good as mine.

So I travel the world in this caravan of mine
But I have to admit it's all in my mind
Because you see this caravan doesn't belong to me
And I'm only here a week, with my friends and me
Holidays abroad, yes, I've done that too
And maybe next year, I will be there like you
But really to be in a far away place
Couldn't bring a bigger smile to this smiling face.

Ann Harford

HEAVEN'S NOT WHAT IT SEEMS

The sun rose dreaming from its sleep,
The shadowed moon did fade.
Still blinking, daylight rose its head,
Another day was made.

Beneath the sky a stranger sleeps,
Through dreaming oceans sails,
His eyes fly open with a crash,
A train of thought derailed.

In greeting birds erupt in song,
The meadow grasses stir,
With certainty, the stranger knows,
He's seen it all before.

Surrounded by perfection, still,
He sees through cynic's eyes,
Another day in paradise,
Devoid of all surprise.

Breathing in the morning air,
He answers with a scream,
'Beware of what you wish for,
Even Heaven's not what it seems.'

M Cobbold

ALL FOR NOWT

When I was a young maid, and just left school,
A shade of green and such a fool,
Missed education to work on the land,
Dry as leaves was my hardened hands.
From dawn till dusk, us did the work,
We farm workers could never shirk.
For a pittance us worked real 'ard,
Milking cows, cleaning the yard,
Cutting grass for silage, or spuds to eat,
Harvesting crops for the winter feed.
Making hay, stacking bales,
Our misguided loyalty never failed.
Feed the calves, plough up fields,
Sowing seeds for the highest yield.
A quick 'alf hour, us 'ad for break,
Never a minute more to make us late.
Cold, heat or rain, us tarried on,
With all them animals us did belong.
Treated 'em right, as if they were our own,
Never 'ad time to whinge and moan.
That ol' farmer, us remembers him well,
Ee should 'ave swapped places for a spell.
Wavin' his stick, no kindness at all,
Red in the face, he would holler and bawl.
Ee has retired now, and living rich,
Us still be working in that ol' ditch.
One day life's battle, us will 'ave won,
Someday justice will be done.

Jane Rennie

DREAMS OF THE PAST

As I strolled through our city of Hereford
It was August and just before noon
Then behold I heard sweet sounds of music
And then I picked out a tune.

Of course it was our Street Organ Festival
I'd forgotten that, bless my soul
I suppose that I could be excused though
After all I am getting old.

As I listened to the notes of sweet music
I was carried away in a dream
To the time when I was a wee small lad
And lots of street organs were seen.

The streets then were not lumbered with traffic
The occasional car would be seen
Or a pony and trap in which the rich person sat
Whilst the times for the poor were quite lean.

Even so most people seemed happy
As their own enjoyment they made
All hours that God sent my father would work
Just for the pittance it paid.

I finally awoke to the present
And slowly took in the scene
I was back in the land of reality
I had awoke from my wonderful dream.

Hark! Am I hearing correctly?
Or are my ears playing tricks in between?
No, the organ is playing my favourite tune
'When I grow too old to dream'.

I had my dream so I was not too old.

Walter Causer

THE JOYS OF SUMMER

It came upon the morning, gay, the sun a golden ball,
Everything was still, and day, with all its hours did call.
Dragging my weary body round from slumber and a-dreaming
I heard, in my ears, a thunderous sound then my nose,
                                it started streaming.
Oh, no! Thought I and fearful dread descended on me seizing
All the cavities in my head and then I started sneezing.
I sneezed to the north, I sneezed to the south, the east
                                and the west weren't missed.
My teeth, they nearly shot from my mouth and my eyes
                                with tears were kissed.
July had come and with full force the pollen rode the breezes
I didn't know if I'd stay the course as my breath came out in wheezes.
Oh! Not to be in the countryside when the summertime is there,
I could hide from the bull, I could hide from the cow but the
                                wasp would find me where
A picnic I had spread on the ground with yummy cakes and goodies,
Then, suddenly, I'd hear the sound of a thousand wing-clad bodies.
If I just took the top off my lemonade or let jam run down my fingers
Into my lap would land a brigade of stripy-shirted stingers.
I'd sit by a wall with my head in my hands feeling somewhat sadder
When through a crevice slithers the form of a fearsome V-headed adder.
All is not peace in the countryside as romantics would have you think,
You pass a farm and if the weather's warm you daren't breathe in
                                for the stink.
But all in all, life's not too bad when you're living out in the sticks,
At least, in the evening, when my day's work is done I can hear
                                the clock when it ticks.
No traffic noise or disco beat, no street lights glaring, yellow,
Only the occasional hoot from an owl and the bull's
                                full throated bellow.

Carol Wright

CONFUSION

Where is my soul? Where is my heart?
Am I in control? Or am I falling apart?
Some senses are numb, and some are alive
But I need them all so I can survive.
I need my feelings to be the truth
But can I trust them, to guide me through?
I sometimes feel weak when I need to be strong
Then I need your guidance so I don't go wrong.
Where is my destiny? It is here? Is it now?
Is it in the future? Or have I missed it somehow?
Could I be happy? Or am I so sad?
For things I've missed and wished I'd had
What's the direction? Which turn to I take?
Will it be the right move? Or the biggest mistake?
Well, not to worry, as they say
I'll finish my poem now and go away.

Ailsa Baillie

AT THE CROSSROADS

Hot and humid is the day as impetus arrives
But I stand rooted to the spot where indecision thrives
Impulsive inactivity! And a tightening in my chest
There's no escape from gravity on looking east to west

There's a chance to be decisive which I'm finding hard to seize
It's impossible to reason without a cooling breeze
All utterance is stifled by the dryness in my mouth
There's oppression in the haze on surveying north and south

To be resolute in mind and transparent with ambition
Would be everything I'm not - and that's a brave admission!
So another opportunity is smothered by constraint
Subdued by limitations that serve without complaint

. . . Refreshing is the evening as nonchalance arrives
And I'm still rooted to the spot where indecision thrives . . .

Matthew Turpin, Ormskirk

OLD ENGLAND

When the snow falls on old England
and it's laying very deep
all the traffic comes to a standstill
and there's chaos in the streets
but for all the little children
they just laugh and shout with glee
for them it's just a fairyland
all gleaming white and neat
they can build a nice big snowman
a castle or a house
or start a fight with snowballs
with nothing to worry about
but the people in little motor cars
all grumble, groan and grouse
while all their little motor cars
just slide and slip about
so if you are ever
in old England, when the snow lays very deep
it will open your eyes
even make you smile
or maybe's make you weep.

Wagtail

CRASH

Tyre stains on tarmac. The blue flashing lights. Emergency services work on through the night.
A slow stream of traffic drives eerily by, as a policeman with white gloves moves them steadily on.
Slowly their heads turn, their windows wind down. Trying to see who lies dead on the ground.
Beneath the red blanket that hides them from view. Glad it was not them who were next in the queue.
Was it someone they knew? Maybe from work or from school? As a fireman cuts metal, sparks fly from the tool.
As the ambulance moves on and the siren grows dimmer. And the police and the firemen clear the debris away.
Red stains on the seats soak the carpets and the doors, it splatters the windscreen and drips onto the road.
I can feel as I lay here my life draining away. It's a high price I pay for speeding today.
The twisted black metal, once my pride and joy, has turned out to be the most deadly of toy.
As family and friends gather round by my grave, some praying, some crying, some turning away. All fearing the same fate will smite them one day.
Now the sun warms the earth which covers my bones and lifts the scent from the lilies on a light summer breeze.
The last smells I recall are of petrol and smoke. As I struggle for freedom, I panic and choke.
I thought I was safe as I sat in my Porche. So smug at the envious glances I caught.
I can see it so clearly, as if from afar . . . oh God! I wish I'd stayed home now and polished the car.

Ian Jackson

HOME TO STAY

I cried a tear when I left today, it trickled down my face,
I held her hand and kissed her lips as she sent me on my way,
I crossed the Tyne bridge and blew her a kiss, she caught it
                                              with her eyes,
She placed it deep inside her heart as she whispered 'Mike, goodbye'
My teardrops fell like raindrops drowning the pain within
Tho' we did part upon this day we promised to meet again.
We'll meet upon this majestic Tyne bridge, when weeks
                                               turn into years,
With love and patience in our soul with secrets we both share.
Then I'll look into gentle eyes, and smile the tears away,
I'll whisper softly into her ears,
Darling at last I'm home to stay.

Elizabeth Patterson

CAMPING BY LOCH AR'N

Ground level clouds swirling and mixing with Loch Ar'n as
Rain sleeting in from the east tears the air from my lungs
Wind screeching and howling around crags and rock towers
Water roaring down the gullies like a never-ending turbine
Then the fight with wet canvas to make shelter for the night
Now safe and snug the aroma of hot food eases the fright
Later, oh much later, a calm descends: winds fall, stars twinkle
Soon it's a cold still night as a frost creeps over the ground
All is still, you sleep not knowing that a white blanket
                                               is covering your world.

Roger Coates Smith

Eternity

Sitting by the fireside watching its golden glow
The wind a mournful sound the air is laced with snow
Place your arms around your wife, tell her that you care
And watch the firelight glow sparkle in her hair
That was once as bright as any summer's day,
                 still bright but now laced with grey
The years have gone by as quickly as the driven snow
And still love each other as only they can ever know
Hold each other's hand as they have done many times before
These later years will pass quickly by and will be no more
Their love and life in this world soon will never be
It will be in another world and for all eternity.

B Wood

Summertime

How I wish summertime would come to stay
So I could brush the cobwebs out of the way.
Flowers taking their first peek
Sunshine and petals with their warmth they seek.
Glistening with early morning dew
To awake the silent few.
Everglades so golden and green
Such a delight to be seen.
Once more the seasons come around
With all the beauty growing out of the ground.

A Dutschak

MARY

My wish is not upon a star
Is not so near, yet not so far.
It is to be forever with her
My radiant queen and no other.

She my beauty of spirit and soul.
She my lady who fills every role.
I ache, my heart aches to break
I offer my life for her to take.

She my ruby, my pearl, my sapphire
My beloved queen of heart's desire.
Majestic in blue, her sovereign lace
I yearn for her love, her sweet embrace.

Long ago, ages past, cloaked in red.
She watched her son de-robed and bled.
Her tears for Him that never dried
Her heart upon the cross, her Son crucified.

Her spirit of love, of peace, of joy.
She remembered those days when He was a boy.
The Word outstretched, His body a smother
'Woman your son, son your mother.'

My mother, my queen, my lady in waiting.
Patiently, loving, tenderly baiting.
Every breath of life drawn within.
To praise, worship and exalt her King.

Edward Joseph Clark

MARRIED LIFE IS A WONDERFUL THING

Married life is a wonderful thing
As two people together it does bring
It brings happiness and love
With the help of our Lord above
Together, making their first home
From which they will never roam
Together, sharing the work
From which they will never shirk
Buying nice things for their house
They never grumble or grouse
Then, maybe after about two years
Their first baby is music to their ears
Another mouth to feed will be no bother
It will be alright to his father and mother
And as the years roll by
The baby is now a nice big boy
Then he will be going to school for the first time
He really looks smart and so fine
Growing up, he is fifteen
Much joy and happiness they have seen
Mother and father getting older
Their boy, so brave and bolder
Getting his first job in a furniture store
Who could ask for much more
And, as the years roll on
They are so proud of their son
They have had such a happy life
The son, husband and wife.

C Ducker

REMEMBER ME

He places the bottle
On the doorstep
In prominent view,
Before shutting the door
For one last time.

All of the bills are paid,
No family or friends,
So he owes nobody at all,
As he places the noose
Around his neck.
Best quality hemp -
A little luxury,
You only die once
After all.

Nobody at his grave to mourn,
He was no genius
Whose work will be remembered
A thousand years from now,
Nor will he be preserved
Like an Egyptian mummy,
In a museum's glass coffin
For school children to draw.

No, immortality is reserved
For gods and screen stars,
His suicide note in the milk bottle
May be discussed for a while,
With ghoulish relish
'Til something new happens,
And he'll be relegated
To the lost memory bin.

Clare A Lewis

ENNUI DES ENFANTS

What shall I do today, Mother,
To stave off boredom's ills?
I've done my homework, cut the grass
And watered the daffodils.
I do find boredom awful, Mum,
For it gives me a terrible itch;
To save me scratching I run a mile
Then I get such a painful stitch.

There's lots of things you could do, my child.
You could take up floral display
Or you could try to write a poem
If you've something worthwhile to say
And then, of course, when it's dark and clear
You could gaze at a twinkling star
And ponder the word Humility
And wonder just what you are.

Frank Sutton

3RD MARCH 1972 (AFTERMATH)

Well the day has come
And the day has gone.
We ate our dinner
We sang our song.

Dinner was nice
Wine was cold.
She was beautiful
And she was sweet.

Time made us tired
Nowhere to go.
Homeward we went
Tea we drank.

I only wish I knew
If my love for you is true.
But what is the difference
I'm sure we are through.

P Mannion

TODDLER TRIP

Look at the time,
It's hardly worth
Going,
Hurry up,
No. You don't need that,
Well all right take it,
- Yes take it,
Now stop crying,
Are you going to stop?
Perhaps you'd better stay,
Bye-bye, I'm going,
Wail!
Well are you coming?
Yes,
Wipe your face,
I don't know why I take you anywhere,
By the time we get out of the door . . .
Slam!

Cathy Saunders

I Do Notice

Do you know what I see, Phylis, Do you know what I see?
Do you know what I'm thinking, when I'm looking at you?
I don't see a crabbit old woman who isn't very wise,
I see a young soul who knows what life is,
Who knows how to live it, who thinks it's the biz.
I know you know, exactly where you are,
When I speak to you your eyes don't seem as far.
You don't mean to dribble your food,
Or go into that mood, it just happens.
When you don't reply, I know why,
When your eyes aren't with us,
You're dreaming of flying high,
High above the clouds which linger in the sky,
That's when I say come on, please try.
I know what you're doing,
I've seen you when you've lost that stocking or shoe,
Because I was the one who found it - not you.
Why don't you get bad tempered, or stroppy,
When I feed, bath and dress you,
Or take you to the loo.
You confuse me - yes, you do.
When I look into your eyes,
I start to wonder if that's you,
As I look closer I can see,
The stages of your life,
When you were six, ten and twelve,
Then your teenage years, from thirteen to twenty,
When you made a mistake, and ended up with a child,
Your love for that child is strong yet mild.

The father of the child,
Becomes the partner at your side,
As you walked down the aisle you took a big stride,
As you make up thirty,
Your child it has changed,
From the nappies that were dirty,
To being star-struck with fame.
Now you are forty, your child it has gone,
At fifty you enjoy a cup of tea and a scone,
And now your child has a child of its own,
To love and to care for and build a secure home.
The years that you look at, you look at with dread,
As you see that at sixty your husband is dead.
Your heart it did crumble when they left you with me.
Inside that battered body,
Is a young girl who longs to be free.
As you think about this your smile changes to a pout,
When you look back on the years your smiles leaps back out,
As you think of the husband who brought you the child,
Now you think that the years went by too fast.
And now you have realised that nothing will last,
Because sooner or later it all becomes the past.
I know who you are Phylis . . . You're you.

Lauren Nield (14)

MAD COW

Running, running round the field
Screaming, shouting *Mooo*
Bucking, kicking on his back
When everyone thinks he's gone to bed
Stuffing himself with lots of grass
Black and white blurred in the field
Aahhh! Splat!

Alice Sanders (6)

YOUR STAR SHINES ON ME

Your words they hold me when I'm alone and in need of a friend.
Your voice it calms me when I'm feeling unsteady.
You were not the first but, you could be the best thing
                                that ever happened to me.

All the colours that fill up my skies seem to remind me of you.
All the songs you sing and play may have come from heaven.
You were not the first but, there will never be another you.

Your star shines on me and lights the way ahead that was dark before.
You have a way that I try to describe, but these words always
                                        seem to fail me.
Have you been sent to take me away from these shady
                                and strange places?

I turned the corner into another street and you knocked me off my feet.
I dreamt of you that night, you knew my name, not a word was spoken.
You are one in a wide world, but to me you fill up all of the
                                        northern skies.

You shine in a hue of yellow, with arms that come to wrap around
                                        when I'm cold.
Your smile is all I need to brighten up my day, it lingers
                          long after you've gone.
You are the everything and you don't even know it. Let it be me
                                        that tells you.

I'm gonna tell the world that it's you I want to be with,
                          I will shout it loud.
I'm feeling like a king today, I don't need a robe or crown to prove it.
You could be my dream love; I hope that I'm not dreaming
                                      this time around.

You were not the first, but there will never be another quite like you.

Clive Louis Turvey

WE ARE THE LUCKY ONES

To live by the sea; like me
On a day such as this
Is a chance not to be missed
To walk on the prom and look for someone
Amidst a sea of happy smiling faces
All out for the day, enjoying places
Far from home towns so dull and grey
Watching people out at play
Far away from homes
From towns of brick and stones
Wearing a 'Kiss me quick' hat
And renting a flat
Enjoying hot-dogs on the promenade
And rides on the 'Big One' what a charade!
They come to sunbathe on the beach
And to paddle though often the tide is out of reach
For most of the day
But we are here to stay
For this is our home town
We see it up, we see it down
But they are only here for a holiday
And we are here to stay
So when they go home far inland
We can walk hand in hand
And enjoy the pleasure that it brings
As our heart sings
And a windblown seashore
Is something to adore.

Joan King

PIGS

I must protest, I really must at the
Slandering of pigs,
At the unkind innuendoes and cruel
Little digs.
For to say that they are ignorant
And grovel in the dirt,
Is a slanderous remark indeed,
One guaranteed to hurt.
Of course they are glutton . . . eous,
Their manners are most atroc . . . ious,
And yes they lack the niceties of life,
But so is the rhinoceros,
So big and slow and ponder . . . ous,
And the clumsy hippopotamus,
Whose manners equal those of any pig!
And what about the octopus,
Whose behaviour is obnox . . . ious,
Who would eat you given half a chance!
There are many other species too,
Some not even in the zoo,
Whose manners would put any pig to shame,
Though it would be indec . . . oriuos,
Considered most deplor . . . ious
If ever we were to mention them by name.
So when next you wish to criticise,
Your neighbour on the other side,
And make audacious judgements,
As we very often do,
Just pause and try to visualise
How it would look in your eyes
If pigs were to extemp . . . orise
And tell the world what they might
Think of you!

E Collins

CRACKERMAN

Crackerman
loses control
talks to his shadow
dancing like flames
roll away, far away.

Out of danger
out of sight
roll away.

He raises his hands
to stir-fry a storm
a Siamese smile
to choke on
roll away, far away.

Out of nothing
out of mind
roll away.

Brokenman
leaving home
where does he go
smelling like a rose
roll away, far away.

A Howard

To Goodwood By Way Of Wisborough Green

I had not known what thrills awaited me.
Names, plotted on the map, appeared,
Correct in order too! What satisfaction.
Not in being right, but in a reassurance.
So much of me of late had been in chaos.
The journey started that way too,
And then the madness of the by-pass;
The 'peacock' in the racing car, so keen to show his skills,
Went right, as I went on.
Aloud I spoke, 'Thank God', and then the calm.
So soon, the beauty and the wonder
Of dappled sunlight through trees.
I gasped within me at the beauty all the way;
Sometimes the trees were misty with the elegance of fairyland;
Then crisp with darker greens, as rays of brilliant sunshine
Beamed through to ever-changing scenes.
Spells of open countryside, old towns and villages,
Busy with craft fairs and fetes enriched the way.
Then quite suddenly another bend, and Goodwood,
High, above the Sussex countryside,
So clear in the brightness of the day,
Countryside through which I had just travelled.
Breathtaking views, and in this picture the Cathedral spire,
Simple, elegant, symbolic.
How blessed had been this journey to
Goodwood, by way of Wisborough Green.

Audrey Euangeline

COLNE VALLEY WATERS

Colne Valley waters once ran clear
Before pollution marred the scene.
No sweeter waters I confess
Flowed like the Colne: the Gade and Chess.

When horse-drawn barges in their day
Glided by with silent grace
Along the canal's waterway -
The world moved at a steadier pace.

As a small boy with rod and line
I found places free to me:
There days of angling were sublime -
I dwelt in nature's mystery.

Such life abounded in the reeds,
The vole and coote, the waterhen:
That secret world down in the weeds
I saw in those clear waters then.

That waterworld is hidden now
By pollution's murky screen,
Yet nature still survives - somehow!
But not as it might once have been.

Jack Judd

A Sense Of Timing

I could not see how she could care,
only the glory of her hair,

could not believe I might claim this prize,
only the magnificence of her eyes;

dismissed the notion that I her love could win,
so transfixed was I by the translucence of her skin,

the sensuous way she'd tilt her hips,
the fierce attraction of her lips,
the way her presence illuminated each day.
I had wished she would never go away

but, despite the late, bashful bid,
despite devotion . . . I fear she did -

for, when resolve had done with climbing,
I found I lacked a sense of timing!

Phoenix Martin

Yellow Dogs

They are the thugs
that maim and kill
Their cowardice shining, yellow
full with fascistic fill

They eliminate with hatred
with eyes of malice
Their ignorance spilling, blood
Stupidity their blinding force

They are the imbeciles
who exude nationalistic pride
Their poisonous heads, venomous
As they fire missiles

Demons of dismembered death
Riding the scenes of violence
Disregard love and life
With their vengeful intolerance.

M Eissa

ROLL UP

Come on in,
the grass is lovely,
find music here
to make the day,

there's drums, guitars -
no need to fret -
with songs to take
your cares away.

The searing beat
twins with the sunshine -
to spread the warmth,
attract the crowds,

so come on in,
the grass is lovely,
let's blow away
these boring clouds!

A Clough

RELATIONS AND RABBITS

Gone are the hedges where my granny used to pick blackberries.
My mother spoke of high hedges and no street lights.
When she first came up the road she said she kept to the centre,
Walking alone from the town on the dark autumn night.

They built thirty-six houses on land where four cottages stood.
The road's flanked with pavements and the only danger's from cars!
In fields where Uncle James gathered mushrooms . . . eruptions
                                                    of dwellings,
At dusk myriad glittering street lamps rival the stars.

The shop where my granda fixed shoes is a unisex hairdressers',
What he'd have thought of that I just do not know!
He died of a broken heart two months after my granny
In '63 after the great fall of snow.

My father tied his old raincoat over the bar of his bicycle
To make a seat for me when he took me to school.
I always feared Loughreys' geese would advance on us hissing,
What a relief when they kept to the field and the pool!

That was the field where the wild rabbits played.
My father said their traditional run
Was through the convent grounds and past the church,
Round to the graveyard to bask in the sun.

That's where they all lie now, my parents, my uncle . . .
And my grandparents have been there since I was thirteen.
I'm anchored to this town, my roots grow deep,
Changed though it is I love it more than any other place I've seen.

Sometimes in the cemetery on warm summers' evenings
I see a wild rabbit asleep on the grass.
It darts off at the mere sound of my footstep,
A haunting, unchanging glimpse of the past.

Clare McAfee

Morgan The Shepherd And His Wife

Morgan the shepherd and his wife,
Looked after sheep with faces black as night,
They lived on the mountains,
Where you could hear ripples of fountains,
He opened the door, three men stood on the grassy hill top floor,
They told him that they travelled a very long way,
They were expected home that very day,
He gave them some food and a drink of ale,
They stopped looking so very pale
They sat him down by the warm, warm fire
They asked what is your heart's desire,
He said to play the harp and sing,
If that is what you want then that is the thing,
He ran his fingers along the strings,
They made sweet notes like ting, ting, tings.

Lucy Gallilee (10)

What Is It About You?

What is it about you
That makes me feel this way?
What is it about you
That brightens up each and every day?
What is it about you
Makes me fall to my knees and pray?
What is it about you
That takes my very breath away?
What is it about you
That leaves nothing left to say . . .
Only that it is *just* you
And everything about you
Because I love you.

Angela McLaughlin

ASSERTIVENESS

Being assertive, it seems to me
Is the way we all should be,
Being assertive takes more time,
'Time is money' taking time is a crime?

Or is it? Because in the end,
Your opponent becomes a 'friend',
Not holding a grudge, but feeling understood,
Surely that's got to be to the good.

Being aggressive or passive can eat you away,
Hanging on to all that grief cannot make your day,
So don't let things fester, you really must let go,
Forget it and start again, that's the only way to grow,

Assertiveness can make life more fulfilling,
It surrounds us with people that are more willing.
It may just take a little longer,
But in the end we'll all be stronger.

It's ammunition and armour rolled into one,
Something hits, you deal with it, let go and it's gone,
Knowing you're armed for the world outside,
Dealing with it caringly gives you pride.

It's a power that doesn't hurt,
It's there to strengthen bonds,
It's a tool to find the truth,
So it can't be wrong.

Sue Barnes

THE PLACE IN WHICH WE LIVE

A fairyland, a gingerbread house,
And where are the gingerbread people?
They're not so hard to find.
A dreamland with smiling faces;
Beams of satisfaction? Maybe
Curiosity? Maybe two smiles for each face -

A castle, a palace, but who's to be
The ruler? The pawns and knaves mill
Through doors until no more doors appear.
A fantasy, a whirlpool of non-entities
Where gingerbread people float and
Bathe in their existence.

A doll's house, a rocking horse
Where the saddle is worn and weak,
While the dolls sit back with
Glass eyes and putrid grins.
A yellow brick road where each brick is
Grinning at each foot that treads it -
Tread softly, gingerbread folk,
A fairyland is a jumbleland with
Magic in the air . . .

M M Forshaw

A Birthday Blessing

February days are often glum,
When icy winds turn fingers numb,
And old man winter sends the snow,
It's nature's way to help things grow.

But if you look closely you will see,
Young green buds on many a tree,
And the little snowdrop starts to thrust,
Her tender shoots through winter's crust.

So when we bemoan this time of year,
With all the problems it may bring,
It's old man winter's last farewell,
Before the start of *spring*.

Then as the dark clouds start to break,
And the winter sun breaks through,
Mother nature starts to wake,
And turn the grey skies into blue.

When your birthday is this time of year,
Then you are truly blessed,
And may good fortune follow you,
This day, and all the rest.

J Knott

MY THOUGHTS

The world, the world
what a funny thought
just like a child waiting to be taught.
Full of wonder, full of thought,
full of things that it's been taught.

The sea, the sea. What can it be?
A giant puddle? A giant tear?
Just wait to see what you will hear
while standing on the pier.

The land, the land, that is on what we stand.
It's hard, it's soft, it's wet, it's dry.
But it's a million miles
away from the sky!

The sky, the sky, what is it right up high?
There it is hanging around
will it ever come to the ground?
Does it feel nice? Does it make a sound?
I don't know it's not near to ground!

Light, light. Why is it so bright?
A light bulb, the sun.
Light can be fun.
Light from stars, light from Mars
but light will never be ours!

Sound, sound. It's all around!
All the words that people have said
have all run through my head!
Where would we be without sound?
I know just looking around.

Jade Hughes (13)

Autumn

The autumn now crowds in about us
Bringing with it colours bright
All the berries hang in clusters
Sometimes dark and sometimes bright
As the days draw ever inward
And the nights grow cold and long
Birds keep singing and they're winging
Heavenward, homeward, still on song.
Slowly now the winter's coming
Bringing with it frost and snow
Days are shorter, nights are longer
Fires need kindling - brighter glow
Now the days begin to lengthen
And the earth begins to stir
Flowers are growing, trees are showing
Mother nature does her work
Soon we'll see that vast arrangement
Of the greatest show on earth.

Pamela J New

My Rocking Chair

Oh, how I love my old rocking chair, truly a relic of the past,
It's been 'done up' so many times, in order to make it last,
I really would like it to outlast me,
So through my old age, I'll rock comfortably.

It's been 'sanded down' and varnished with pride,
Had a new seat which is woven inside,
Parts coaxed back together, with a wooden hammer,
Used as much by me, as my old grand-mamma.

I could never part with it, I love it so much,
And it's old 'soft feeling' wood, I love to touch,
When I'm tired it's the one place I can nod off so easy,
It's also my salvation if I'm feeling queasy.

A few little rocks, and my eyelids are closing,
With the greatest of ease, I'm soon reposing,
When I awake, it's such a comfort to me,
Realising I am, where I want to be.

Eileen Handley

WOODS

Woods have secrets,
whispering, wind-soughing,
softly sifting
filtering sunlight,
winding the tree-ways,
riding the streams,
rushing, fading,
hushing their dreams.

Woods are restless,
ringing with secrets
even when silent -
now, can't you hear them?
They would draw you
into their dreaming -
what then of *your* secrets?
Would they heed *your* dreams?

And how would it be by moonlight,
or in the unlit night?

G Nussbaum

SOLITUDE

A trickle of a tiny stream,
One single blade of grass.
Bird of song, way on high -
Solitude, I sigh!

Sheep in a flock
Some gate with no lock.
Sun's dappling rays -
Shimmer o'er the lake.

Two herons a-fly.
Swiftly darting a
Kingfisher in pretty hue.
Peace by and by.

Margaret E Preston

MY LOVE FOR YOU

I've a very special love
that's meant for you alone,
something very special
that only you can own.
I cannot find the words
to say just how I feel,
but I know my darling
my lips I cannot seal.
I have to tell the world
how much I love you so,
there may be no tomorrow
so how will they ever know?

Margaret Jean Wilcock

TRUTH

The truth of truth is this, that truth is fire
And fire will burn and fling around its light
And light will pierce with unchecked sense of might
And drive out darkness and my sense of fear
So I can live and love as I aspire.
But light which drives out shadows, puts to flight
My sense of broken ease, which makes me fight
To seek the truth and so I'm the loser.
But truth itself is also lost, because -
The light of truth outshines the shade of doubt
And without doubt there is no spur to seek
The truth, and so it burns away the boughs
And turns to ash what little truth there might
Have been, to spark the flame, to give me light.

'Truth is fire, and fire means to illuminate and to burn' (L Scheffer).

David James

SNOWMAN

The snowman's going,
the snowman's going,
the sun came out today,
we built it oh so very high
and now it's dripped away,
we thought it would last a million year,
my mum said it would stay,
but when the sun came out today,
it took him all away.

Kathy Watson

THE BAD CHAIR

There was Tiny sitting sad
On that bad chair;
A forlorn look upon her face
And tension filled the air.

Have you been bold again
I mused in gentle voice;
Aye, she blushed and sobbed
Not once but nearly twice.

I kissed her forehead soft
Between the straggling hair;
But you've been good besides
As she wriggled in the chair.

With cheeks so flushed up pink
And her little feet turned in;
A dolly held before her face
She sneaked a little grin.

Dressed up pretty in a frock
And with that friendly smile;
How could this wee innocent
Hide so much craft and guile.

She is now a little lady
With abundant charm and grace;
Is this a victim of that chair?
Is this that smiling face?

John F McCartney

HANDS

Those gnarled hands are tired, swollen and sore
As they lie in the lap of their owner
No longer can they knit or sew
No longer are they able
They have worked for a lifetime at all sorts of jobs
Too much to do to take care of them
The children came and had to be reared
There was scrubbing and washing and baking
There were no electric mixers then
No washing machines or dishwashers
And being a farmer's wife these hands
Had to give a hand with the milking
There were calves to rear and pigs to feed
Pet lambs to attend in their season
Hens to feed and water and eggs to clean
As well as a flock of turkeys
There were times when sickness took up her time
But with it all she was able
To give a hand in the bog for a day
Or help with the corn or potatoes
I raise my hat to the farmer's wife of the past
She did all without much complaining
Her reward was to see her family do well
This was the driving force behind her.

John McGowan

AMORAL DILEMMA?

I'm very hard to please, dear wife,
Only the best will do.
We only have one precious life
To make our dreams come true.

Nagging demands and constant whines
Make not a happy home.
Can't you read between the lines,
Those blonde hairs in the comb?

That silk shirt with the new tie,
The new sexy underwear,
Don't you ever ask him why?
Maybe you don't dare.

Don't rest on your laurels
Or think you've seen it all.
Never believe the lies he tells,
I'm waiting for his call!

Geraldine McIlmurray

THE BUTTERFLY

How beautiful its colours, as it flits from bloom to bloom,
It pollinates the flowers deftly, like a weaver's fingers on the loom,
So lazily it flutters, until deciding where it wants to lay,
Then settles for what seems an age, before going on its way.
The eggs are hatched quite quickly in the brightly shining sun,
And caterpillars soon are seen and the cycle has begun.
For nature's metamorphosis, is so wonderful, oh my!
From the hairy caterpillar, comes the lovely butterfly.

L Barnes

INVENTION

When we look around the farm today
There's much that we can find,
We must admit to rapid strides,
Bygones are left behind.

No longer do we stand and watch
The horse and plough together.
So tractors hum and buzz and drive
In every kind of weather.

Too slow, too slow, the farmer says
Milk cows by hand - not me.
So off to the milking parlour they go,
Where machines work speedily.

The hens and chicks no longer roam
As they did in bygone ages,
Alas in prison they spend their days
Like machines - they lay eggs in cages.

Invention in every field we see
No matter what we take
Much hard work has been left behind
'Tis good, for each one's sake.

But the latest invention, in final stages,
Is what I'm longing to see,
When the duck by its intake is made to lay,
Striped eggs for my tea.

Nell Thompson

WINTER ON THE FARM

Across the fields the snow lay thick,
With hedges all covered in white,
Through his window the old man looked,
And thought 'What a beautiful sight'.

The barn that sheltered his old horse,
In the snow appeared to be new,
But in his heart he knew quite well,
Of planks it was missing a few.

The path he had to tread each day,
Was covered in snow all the way,
He knew he had to fetch the logs,
And feed his old pal come what may.

The old farm house was very cold,
He thought 'If I'd had gas laid on,
At the time the farm was thriving,
I'd be warm tho' my money's all gone'.

When it was dark he went to bed,
The blizzard raged all through the night,
Next morning when he looked outside,
He thought 'What a terrible sight'.

He knew his horse had to be fed,
That was a job he could not leave,
So out into the storm he went,
His horse's hunger to relieve.

After that the farmer returned,
To sit by his now glowing hearth,
Thankful he needn't go out again,
To walk down that treacherous path.

Isobel Crumley

MOUTH LIKE A ROSE

I spied you first as I sat down
The sunlight bright had dimmed my eyes,
Sea breezes through my hair had blown
Self-conscious I felt my colour rise
Bowing my head, my thoughts were jangled
Trying to think, what could I say?
As usual I'd sneaked in the seat furthest back
And beautiful you so far away.
The sun slanting through the coloured glass
Caught the shine on your hair, I wanted to touch
Me, I don't suppose you'd notice in the mass
I longed for your eyes to meet mine so much
It was hard to concentrate on the speaker
When out of the blue, you smiled at me
My arms ached to hold you, my legs felt weaker
Heart fluttering, I craned my neck, your beauty more to see
Your cheeks like satin, your mouth like a rose
And then, oh then! Your eyes started to *close*
As we sang the last hymn, your dad raised you up on his shoulder
Sweet baby, you and sweet Jesus
Has made this old world a little less colder
For people like me (left alone) when we're older.

Millicent B Colwell

LAND OF MY DREAMS

How can I describe the land of my dreams to you?
Except to say, away from urban areas,
As you travel round each bend, wonderful scenery comes into view
Enhanced in the spring by the golden yellow of the gorse in bloom,
Whilst in the autumn bracken of burnished orange and red
Mingled with purple heathers covers the open ground,
For Scotland holds open its door for you all to see around
And her people will welcome you with, 'Hello, how are you,
                                    come in for a while, won't ye.'
How can I describe the majestic grandeur of the mountains,
The stunning beauty of the lochs and lochans,
The golden and silver sands of unblemished beaches,
The shades of blue, green and turquoise of the sea.
The peace, quiet, solitude and tranquillity?
Then there's the warm friendliness of her people,
The pride and loyalty to the land,
The sense of history as you visit not just towns and cities
                                    but the countryside too,
What I love about this country I cannot describe on paper to you,
It's in my heart, it's in my mind, it's in my very soul
This country that I visit but have never lived,
This country that is very, very special to me,
And in truth, is where I long to be.

Lesley Stevenson

COME TO THE FAIR

Come to the fair, the jolly old fair
Let's join in the fun with everyone there
The music so grand makes you want to dance
You feel so happy, you're in a trance

The roundabout horses looking so grand
Galloping round to the sound of the band
All coloured lights a fairyland we love
The moon and the stars shine down from above

Up high on the wheel come screams of delight
Are all mixed together with some of sheer fright
The dodgems are a favourite treat
It's great with a girl in the next seat

So to the side-show to try our luck
A go on the rifle range to knock down a duck
To try for a coconut is good fun
Then for refreshments, some tea and a bun.

It's late, so homeward we go
But it's been grand, we've enjoyed it so
The fun and laughter, the night has flown
Our trip to the fair's been the best we have known.

G Emery

VICTIMS OF CIRCUMSTANCE

Red brick,
stone stairs,
cold nights,
blank stares.
Draughty halls,
distempered walls.

Outcasts -
From the workhouse.

Society's dispossessed.
Often clean,
never best dressed.
Often hungry,
never quite starved.

Outcasts -
From the workhouse.

Many tears,
born of fears
brought on by uncertainty.
When,
all we wanted
was to be
an 'ordinary' family.

Eventually, our wish came true,
one of many, not one of few -
a house, a home, and happily,
accepted by society.

Now that I am 'middle class'
I never talk about my past,
because -
I know,
the stigma lasts.

Outcasts -
From the workhouse.

Elizabeth A Rice

LIGHTHOUSE

A cloudy night
Obscured by mist
A beam's bright light
Guides ships away
From rocks' outcropping fists

Some lonely life
To stand a sentry
Saving men from strife
A guiding light, a helping hand
So stopping their deaths entry

On sunlit days
You stand up tall
As people walk their sep'rate ways
Many stop and talk of you
What if you should fall?

If you should fall
Your light extinguished
No more you stand up tall
The rocks unsafe, no more are guarded
Oh lighthouse so distinguished

Gemma Guymer

EAST ANGLIA

East Anglia is very well known,
To thousands of us it is our home.
Wherever we are we are close to the sea,
No need to travel far, a few miles maybe.
We are a caring crowd who live this way,
We talk funny though some folk would say.
Sound like a farmer all countrified,
Ooh arr! Ooh arr! We don't try to hide.
But we don't all have straw stuck out of our mouth,
And the manure, the fresh air is good for our health.
We still have cities and some towns,
So don't look down you nose and put us down.
We have Ipswich Town and Norwich City,
So it's not all scenic more's the pity.
But we have a famous poet called Sally Swain,
So East Anglia makes yet another victory claim.

Sally A Swain

CASABLANCA

I was watching the famous film one afternoon,
and by the end, I cried like a fool!
Was it the story? Was it the gloom?
No! It reminded me of something wonderful!
Every week we would go to London town!
At that time the 'movies' were films!
The acting was perfect and so was the sound!
Humphrey Bogart and Ingrid Bergman were our dreams!
We loved the song 'As time goes by'
And the atmosphere of the last war!
Like Bogart and Bergman, we said goodbye!
But instead of Paris, we had London once more!

Romana Bartosiak

A Message From Mom

My sweet mom called today
And she said 'Your Dad loves you,
I know it now,
He just doesn't know how to relate to you
Because you are like me.
He has a lot of love in him.
He does not know how to share it
But I will help him, and let him know,
He has a daughter
Who is part of him
Who wants him to be proud.
I'll let him know, because now I can
Because I am here, in heaven
And it is beautiful, like my valley.
I miss you, and I am with you,
When you call.'

Lynn Jean Barry

Sunday

Think back to the Sundays of yesteryear
And the pattern of life that we held so dear
For us it was always a time to find rest
Then face the next week with a greater zest
The churches ring bells, they are not calling us
We just pass them by in a car on a bus
The shops are now open down every road
This is good commerce or so we are told
Those bright happy times have now gone forever
For we never will get the family together
So let us hold fast to this precious day
A treasure is lost if we take it away.

M Walker

Mr Nobody

He visits our house every day,
And roams around with glee.
In fact I think he's come to stay,
That Mr Nobody.

The pens and pencils disappear,
He even spills the tea
And leaves the toys out on the floor,
That Mr Nobody.

He puts the lights on,
Moves the tools,
And eats cakes saved for tea,
He's never known to shut a door
Our Mr Nobody.

He'll hide a shoe, a purse or comb,
Or even take a key,
I really wish he would go home
That Mr Nobody.

Maybe he'll come to visit you
And yet we all agree,
The house just wouldn't be the same
Without Mr Nobody.

Joyce Mussett

To A Dragonfly

How skilfully you fly.
I watched you come and then pass quickly by.
I wondered where you were going to land
felt quite honoured when you settled on my hand,

and while you were perched there
I studied your lace-like wings
one of nature's
remarkable things.

Were you a skipper
or a darter or hawker
were you the one
who dive-bombed that walker?

James V Hooton

Yesterday

When petals fall and butterflies end their flights
and the wind wafts over the meadow
it reminds me of yesterday and the purple-blue heather.
When days were long, and oh so slow,
we seemed to have time to dream and grow.
Where did it go, the time and the dream?
Washed away in a rippling stream
or locked away, no more to be seen.
The purple-blue heather is still to be found,
the dreams and hopes altered by time
we could have had it all, it could have been sublime
now all that's left is the wind, as the petals fall, as the years unwind.

I D Welch

Mystery Coach Tour

Cushion yourselves on the plush seats,
Rest your heads on the white linen,
And together we will find the by-ways
That are still at the heart of England.

I will take you where the Cotswold heart of England
Draws us through green groves and honey-coloured villages,
I will show you deer parks where dappled does
Lose themselves in dappled shadow.

Grand golden houses where the present meets the past
With a few pounds paid over at the door,
And the perfumed walks and shaven lawns are yours
Till evening, when the great gates clang behind you.

Then through the darkening glory of England
I will take you home, showing you this last
Magnificence, this castle of Warwick
Strongly dark upon its hill against a fiery sky.

And should we pass a field of flame in the darkness
It is neither ancient nor modern battle,
But only a farmer burning stubble
As he has always done in England in September.

Sheila Town

Silent Prayer

Good Lord look down on me
Poor sinner though I be,
From thy throne above
I really need thy love.

So many be the way
I could go astray,
That I might make a stand
I need thy guiding hand.

Wrongful things within the head
Whether thought or said.
Your voice I'd like to hear
To soothe away my fear.

I see evil being done
So feel I may be one
In need of your protection
To ease my apprehension.

For better life there is a need
To abide a holy creed
By everyone, so that then
Your will be done, Amen.

J R Reading

A STEP WANTING

You walk back home
to the salt of the earth.
Back to the place where you forget
narrow wisdom whispers;
and open, behind geniality and hospitality,
are closed doors.

Your formative years
still hang behind the bedroom door.
The same dressing gown, the old bed,
a creak of springs,
where you dream again of boyhood flying
over the rough tops of your hills
acid with greens of sedges, reeds and grasses
till you see the waterlogged field
where you fall; bogged down,
and jolt awake to the pain of a failed marriage
and a misery that won't leave you alone.

The clock ticks downstairs and the moon
still shines through the same window pane.
You remember your scuffed loafing
in an idleness of security, and realise
that since then, fifteen years have sat
on your bones and made them heavy
with worry and disenchantment.

It's not the same anymore. This bed.
This time. This aching.
Even though, the wallpaper pattern,
the angle of moonlight,
their unspoken communications,
have stayed the same all the time you've been gone.

They are blank with understanding.
You lie awake all night,
listening to the room next door.
The small nocturnal sounds made by strangers,
who once had a son.

Susan Roberts

Words

If words could paint a picture
I hope you'd picture mine
I see a field of rich green grass
With many flowers fine
There's daisies white
And buttercups give off a golden hue
Purple vetch, poppies red
And cornflowers of blue
Surrounded by a hedge of May
A blackbird and bough
And in the corner of the field
I see a brindle ewe
A footpath winds o'er distant hills
A cottage stands alone
Sweet smelling clover by the way
A song thrush to greet me and each new day
If words could paint a picture
A blind man then *could* see
The beauty of the countryside
That's home sweet home to me.

Margaret Vinall-Burnett

ANCHOR BOOKS
SUBMISSIONS INVITED
SOMETHING FOR EVERYONE

ANCHOR BOOKS GEN - Any subject, light-hearted clean fun, nothing unprintable please.

THE OPPOSITE SEX - Have your say on the opposite gender. Do they drive you mad or can we co-exist in harmony?

THE NATURAL WORLD - Are we destroying the world around us? What should we do to preserve the beauty and the future of our planet - you decide!

All poems no longer than 30 lines.
Always welcome! No fee!
Plus cash prizes to be won!

Mark your envelope (eg *The Natural World*)
And send to:
Anchor Books
Remus House, Coltsfoot Drive
Woodston, Peterborough, PE2 9JX

**OVER £10,000 IN POETRY PRIZES
TO BE WON!**

Send an SAE for details on our New Year 2000 competition!